POLITICAL THINKING
The Perennial Questions

POLITICAL THINKING
The Perennial Questions

GLENN TINDER
University of Massachusetts, Boston

Little, Brown and Company Boston

LIBRARY OF CONGRESS CATALOG CARD NUMBER: 75-102429

FIRST PRINTING

Published simultaneously in Canada
by Little, Brown & Company (Canada) Limited

PRINTED IN THE UNITED STATES OF AMERICA

To Galen,
son and independent thinker

A Note on the Use of This Book

The same kind of reading that is received by most other books — that is, one without long pauses for reflection, discussion, and writing — should prove of some value with this book. Although the questions are posed without being resolved, they are linked together in a way that makes them a wandering pathway over the terrain of political thought. I believe that by reading this book one can gain a vivid sense of the intellectual state in which political thinking originates.

This book, however, is designed not just to be read but to be used — in class discussions, in term papers, and even in examinations. The questions are set forth not simply to inform students concerning the dilemmas of others but to draw them into dilemmas of their own. And this can be done only if, in addition to reading the book as a whole, they dwell on at least a few of the questions and try to answer them, either orally or in writing. The questions are clearly stated, separated from one another, and numbered, in order to facilitate their being used in such ways.

Using the book in this fashion is perfectly compatible with the traditional requirement that students gain a knowledge of major theories. In dealing with the questions a student can be required not only to take positions of his own but also to display familiarity with the positions taken by great thinkers of the past and the present. Some of the principal views of these thinkers are described in the presentation of the questions. But this is done with a brevity and selectiveness that leaves ample room for further study on the part of the student.

To aid the student in studying other theories while developing his own, a brief bibliography appears at the end of each chapter. Countless works bear on questions of the breadth that are posed; hence the bibliography is quite selective and personal. It is made up primarily of classics in the history of thought, with a few others added that seem to me of exceptional worth. Also, since most substantial works of political thought deal with a wide range of questions, it has been necessary in some cases to list the same work for several chapters, designating different sections of the work for different chapters; in other cases books which might have illuminated matters discussed in several different chapters were, when not readily divided into sections bearing on these different chapters, listed only in connection with the chapter to which they seemed most relevant. Hence it is an imperfect bibliography. It may nevertheless assist the student in combining reflection with the study of the great thinkers. Only books available in paperback, or in other inexpensive editions, have been listed.

As a further aid, a short appendix on techniques of thought is included at the end of the book.

Readers may find themselves rephrasing some of the questions or asking questions other than those included in the book. This is unavoidable; there can be no final and definitive set of questions. But it does not seem particularly undesirable, since the aim of the book is to engage the reader in intellectual movement. For a reader to be prompted to ask his own questions is hardly less in accordance with the author's intent than for him to develop his own ideas.

Contents

1

Why Engage in Political Thinking?

The purpose of this book is to introduce readers into the area of political thought by presenting and explaining the great questions from which political thought has arisen. Political theory texts are almost universally about doctrines and ideas – about results. The present book is about problems – about beginnings. Each chapter defines and explains a set of related questions. These are left unresolved. The reader, thus, is provided with no conclusions. But this directly expresses the purpose of the book: not to bring the reader to a place of rest but to lead him to positions in which he must think.

This approach rests on the assumption that knowledge of political thought depends on familiarity with the doubts and queries amidst which it is carried on. The process of thought cannot be telescoped into its conclusions without being falsified; for questions are not only the beginning of thought but its continuing environment as well. Ideas and theories that are separated from the problems and questions that prompted their development become intellectual corpses. This is because they become pointless. Hence, live thought is in continuous touch with its underlying questions. This is exemplified in the career of Plato. *The Republic*, the supreme statement of his vision of human life, was composed when he was middle aged; much of his later writing is a questioning of this statement and of its philosophical foundations. What stands out in Plato's life, in addition to qualities like wisdom and imagination, is an irrepressible capacity for reconsideration, for asking again the questions he had already answered. Theories grow in the soil of questions; and just as a full-grown plant needs soil no less than does a first shoot, a fully developed theory remains rooted in questions. A student who is acquainted with the answers, but not with the questions, knows little about political thought.

But there is only one way to learn questions – a second assumption underlying the present approach – and that is to undergo the labor and strain of trying to answer them. For example, one who knows, merely as a matter of historical information, that Plato was concerned with the question of whether political power could be placed in the service of absolute knowledge does not have a real understanding of the question; he can gain that only by asking the question himself and by trying to answer it himself. One cannot become acquainted with political thought from the outside; to study it deeply, one must become actually engaged in it.

Hence, this book concentrates on questions not only because the questions need to be known, but also because they can be known only if they are not too quickly weakened or dissolved by being answered. The usual concentration on ideas risks teaching the student something of thought – a congealed, unchanging deposit – while leaving him ignorant of thinking. In the following pages, to make the questions clear it will be necessary to sketch some of the principal answers they have called forth. But no effort will be made to outline all possible answers or to indicate which of the answers described seem correct to the author.

The main intent of this book is to lead the reader repeatedly to the point at which he must seek his own answers.

All of this, however, suggests that political thinking has only the rather academic value of enabling one to gain a better knowledge of political theories than he otherwise could. This is not a negligible value. Nevertheless, we must ask whether political thinking has more than academic utility. Is there any reason why one should engage in thinking simply because he is a human being and not merely because he is a student of political theory?

One circumstance impelling us to ask this question is that thinking is a peculiarly arduous and discouraging undertaking. Of course, it is often remarked that thinking is difficult. But this statement can lead one to assume merely that hard work is needed in order to reach solid conclusions, whereas one who enters fully into the process of questioning set forth in the following chapters will discover that the difficulties of thinking are far more subtle and exasperating than those of mere hard work. He is apt to find, for example, that the effort of thought at first is completely fruitless; to admit uncertainty, as one must in order to start thinking, often seems to place one in a kind of void, with no horizons in the distance and no solid ground underneath (insight being likely to come unexpectedly, after repeated, apparently futile, efforts to gain it). Further, anyone who tries to think will find himself annoyingly subject to daydreaming and other kinds of mental irresolution. Finally, he will discover that the products of thought are often intangible and fleeting. Ideas that have taken many hours to develop occasionally can be detroyed by a few remarks from a sophisticated friend. All of these conditions mean that a thinking person is exceedingly vulnerable. He must appear before others, not behind the armor and shield of books he has read, but in the nakedness of his own thoughts and doubts.

Nor are the long-range results that come from this precarious and nerve-wracking effort apt to be obviously and unarguably good. It is not manifest that thinking is the way to moral elevation, to happiness, or even to wisdom. Over two thousand years of philosophical doubt and disagreement have proven that it is not the way to unshakable and enduring theories. Undoubtedly something tells many of us that it would be ignoble deliberately to refrain from thinking. But this monitor is not heard by everyone; it was not heard, for example, by as great a writer as Rousseau, who believed that through thinking one suffers degradation.

Finally, contemporary American culture only reinforces the reluctance to think that must arise from these circumstances. Certainly verbal tributes are frequently paid to such goals as "teaching students to think." But most intelligent and cultivated people today do not seem to assign much importance to thought that is of philosophic breadth and seriousness. For example, political scientists might seem to have a special responsibility for political thinking; yet half a century after the end of World War I, which led mankind into the present era of political disorder and violence, there still was not a single political science journal in America devoted wholly, or even primarily, to political philosophy. Further, the behavioralism currently popular among political scientists is overtly antiphilosophical. Broadly similar attitudes seem to reign among the literate public in general. The political books that become widely known are mostly factual and hortatory tracts concerning urgent problems such as the tension between whites and blacks. One of the most important contemporary thinkers, Hannah Arendt, is famous primarily for a topical and relatively unimportant book about Eichmann and the Nazi death camps; her major work of political thought, *The Human Condition,* is little known.

Of course, any society probably has an inherent bias against thought. Social order depends heavily on tradition and habit, and these are apt to be disturbed by real thinking. The execution of Socrates exemplifies this antagonism. Nevertheless, I suggest that today in America two forces, both much stronger than in most times and places, intensify the normal antiphilosophical cast of society and deepen the reluctance of individuals to take on the uneasiness and labor of thought.

The first is a passion to act. Politically conscious people today are tense with the realization of problems that urgently need solving; and they are confident in man's power to solve these problems. This dynamic spirit is of course not bad in all ways, but it makes people impatient with reflection. They seek programs of action.

Accompanying the passion to act, and partly caused by it, is a thirst for facts. Most of us want to know what is actually going on – in the schools, in the slums, in the non-industrial countries. The thirst for facts is, of course, no more inherently reprehensible than is the passion to act. Facts can usually be verified and put to good use; not quite as much can be said of theories. But people who are avid for information are likely to be indifferent to mere thoughts.

In sum, the paths of thought are not altogether inviting. They lead to toil and insecurity, and they do not obviously ever bring one to solid answers and inner rest. Our culture presses on us continually the prior urgency of acting and of gaining reliable information.

Then why – to recur to the title of this chapter – engage in political thinking?

For one thing, some questions cannot be answered in any other way. For example, when does one have the right to disobey the government? Can a government legitimately break moral rules if the welfare of the nation seems to require it? Should all social and economic inequalities be abolished? Questions of this kind cannot be answered without thought. Information bearing on them may come from social science, from personal experience, from history, and from other sources. But only thought can determine what information is truly relevant and then use it in answering the questions.

But must such questions be answered? Cannot one live well enough without ever considering them? The answer to both questions is found in the principle that only through ideas can we discern and enter into relations with reality. An idea is a kind of light; and many of the great political ideas have the double power of indicating not only what is but what ought to be. If it were not for these ideas man's collective existence would be carried on in dusk and darkness.

Thus, for example, it is apparent to most of us that Nazism was fundamentally wrong. But this would not be so apparent were it not for ideas such as the rule of law and the evil of tyranny; and these are not innate in the human mind but were formed by men such as Aristotle, Cicero, and Locke. As another example, to many people today it is as plain as a vast cloud in a noon-time sky that the segregated and inferior position of black people in America is unjust. But from where does the light come that discloses the ominous shape of the social order? Comparable arrangements have prevailed in many societies for thousands of years and have hardly provoked comment; this is exemplified in Aristotle's casual acceptance of slavery. The light in which we view America's racial situation comes from the idea of equality – an idea we probably would not possess had it not been for thinkers such as Locke, Rousseau, and Marx. Perhaps eight or ten ideas are the lanterns of political civilization; they enable us to discern and judge the realities of collective life.

Both the action and the facts prized today in American culture presuppose ideas that can only be formed by thought. To act we must have ends; but ends are simply ideas used for planning action. For example, during the last two centuries men have often protested and rebelled in order to gain the right to participate in the affairs of government. But for several millennia, aside from a few exceptional periods, men acquiesced in the rule of highly exclusive elites. The idea that all men have a right to participate in their government, the spark of much action, could not have been formulated without thought. A similar point can be made concerning the thirst for facts. This thirst is not satisfied by indiscriminately gathering in every fact that happens to be noticed.

Such research would only create a chaos of insignificant and unrelated atoms of information unless it were guided by ideas indicating the relative importance, and the interrelationships, of the facts to be gathered.

Of course, only a few great thinkers create the principal ideas that illuminate reality and guide action and research. But it does not follow that one can accept their ideas without thought, for they offer different, and in some cases mutually contradictory, ideas. How can one decide which ideas to accept without carrying on some thought of his own? Further, even if one were willing to commit himself to ideas instinctively and uncritically, it is doubtful that he could understand them without having experienced some of the labor and doubt that has gone into creating them. What is meant, for example, by the idea that men are equal? Clearly they are not equal in any measurable quality such as intelligence, or health, or emotional balance. One may say that they are equal only in their rights before the law. But why should they be accorded equal rights before the law if they are in no respect equal in fact? The question need not be pursued further in order to show that one who has never reflected on equality can scarcely understand the idea.

Thus, despite our emphasis on questions rather than answers, our first response to the query, "Why engage in political thinking?" is: for the sake of answers that cannot be reached in any other way. This response, however, ignores one of the weightiest and oldest objections to philosophical thought, about politics or any other subject, namely, that the ideas it reaches must always be undemonstrable and uncertain, and that to engage in thinking is to entertain doubts that can never, through thought, be wholly overcome.

I am far from denying that this is so. Few if any of the main political ideas held by a typical American or European at the present time can be proven; most of them can be severely shaken. There are, for example, substantial arguments against even so apparently solid an idea as that of the rule of law. For one thing, as Plato argued, it inhibits full application of intelligence to social problems; for another, in times of bitterness and disorder like the present, it may make it difficult for the police to assure safety of property and person. The reader will probably think of answers to these arguments, but he will not think of any that conclusively refute them. Every important idea is attended by some inseparable counter-ideas. The latter may be weakened in the course of wise reflection, but they cannot be totally destroyed.

The history of political thought shows how doubt continually pursues thought and frequently overtakes it. There is no more agreement concerning political truth now than there was twenty-five hundred years ago, when political thinking began. There may well be less.

Why engage in inquiry of a kind that can only lead to uncertain and disputable conclusions?

At least three responses can be made to this question. The first is implicit in what has been said about the need for ideas that can only be reached by thought. However disputable the conclusions of thought may be, we cannot live in a civilized fashion without them. One may feel it is unsatisfactory that our ideas are so vulnerable to doubt, but it is far better to have doubtful ideas than to have none at all. The former state is uncomfortable but civilized, the latter is barbarous.

The second response is to point out that while every political philosophy has in it a subjective element (for, like a work of art, it is emphatically and thoroughly the creation of a particular person and lacks the impersonal authority of a body of scientific laws), it is not wholly subjective. Put very simply, one cannot believe whatever he chooses. One must conform to the evidence and to the rules of logical consistency. None of the great ideas or philosophies is demonstrably true. But it would be easy to formulate an idea or a philosophy that is demonstrably false, either because it is contrary to unquestioned evidence or because it is internally contradictory. The uncertainty of political ideas should not be exaggerated.

Finally, however, it is worth engaging in inquiry of a kind that can never conquer uncertainty simply for the value inherent in the act of inquiry itself. Through thinking, I suggest, one can gain a sort of humanity that is not available in any other way. What is threatened by the present passion for action and for facts, even though it often expresses an active civic conscience, is a brutalization that is inseparable from thoughtlessness.

What is the nature of the humanity gained through thought?

First of all, one realizes his own free and distinct self-hood. "All deep, earnest thinking is but the intrepid effort of the soul to keep the open independence of her sea." These are the words of Herman Melville in *Moby Dick*. He added that "the wildest winds of heaven and earth conspire to cast her [the self] on the treacherous, slavish shore." [1] Today we may interpret the "treacherous, slavish shore" as a symbol of such enemies of free individuality as ideology, bureaucratic routine, and mass emotion. When one thinks, he stands off from all that is blind and impersonal and automatic. His questions may lead him into confusion, but at least they are testimony that he is a distinct – a free and reflective – being. To study the history of philosophy, religion, and science may lead to the notion that man is not always great in his possession of perfected conclusions; here he is often proud and intolerant. The most moving passages of intellectual history concern periods of exploration and discovery, and these must be periods of doubt and questioning.

Further, through thinking one not only asserts his own distinct selfhood, he also defines it, for thinking is a summoning of the self. When one begins to reflect on a problem of philosophical scope, he must call into consciousness, and test and relate, his strongest impressions and convictions. He must think back on what he has read – in the social sciences, history, literature, and Scripture – and ask what in all of it is reliable and important. He also must consult his own past and ask what he has experienced and felt that should be remembered and taken into

[1] Herman Melville, *Moby Dick, or The Whale* (New York: The Modern Library, 1930), p. 153.

account. Thus, in thinking one is shaping his personal being. This implies that the subjective element in thought – that is, its objective uncertainty – is not purely a drawback. It deprives philosophy of the irresistible power of scientific law; but it enables reflection to play a part in the establishment of a personal identity that scientific research cannot play.

Finally, thought enhances one's humanity by requiring openness to others. All serious and candid reflection is an admission that one may be mistaken. It is also, in some measure, a consideration of the ideas of others. Undoubtedly, strong convictions also have a part in the development of political philosophies. But so far as one thinks, he questions his convictions and thus overcomes the contempt men tend always to feel for parties, nations, and eras with convictions counter to their own. Thus, if by thinking one distinguishes himself from men in their conformity and thoughtlessness, by the same act he joins them in their pitiful uncertainty.

Today we possess awesome powers of action, as manifest in our command of nuclear energy, our penetration into space, and our industrial productivity. We also possess highly developed skills in the accumulation and interpretation of facts, dramatically evident in the scope and refinement of the physical sciences as well as in the vast amount of data accumulated by the social sciences. But it is doubtful that we possess wisdom. Our lives therefore are carried on under an ineffaceable question: Can we make our powers of action and our skills in research serve any valid ultimate purpose? The widespread fear that we may destroy civilization, or even all of life, through nuclear war shows how far we are from being able confidently to given an affirmative answer to this unassuming little question.

I suggest that the wisdom demanded by our powers of action and research does not lie in knowing, beyond all doubt, but in a certain kind of not-knowing – in the uncertainty that expresses both independent selfhood and openness to others. One has a strong yearning for absolute assurance as to what is true and right; one feels his whole identity shaken when his assurance is shaken. But the identity thus imperiled is false. It depends for its realization on certitude rather than thought. This book is based on the premise that man in his finitude and freedom is a thinking being. Hence, one who learns to consider questions with clarity and determination and an open mind gains something that is irreducible to knowledge – the wisdom and poise of humane uncertainty.

2

Estrangement and Unity

If men were not estranged, whether in quiet loneliness or in active conflict, political thinking would not occur. We are impelled to ask about the ultimate forces and standards governing human relations only when those relations are strained and destroyed. Thus the greatest achievements of political thought have for the most part been responses to social disintegration. *The Republic* can be read as a meditation on the Peloponnesian War, in which the Greek cities not only fought one another for several decades but were inwardly torn by ferocious factional conflicts; *The City of God,* by Saint Augustine, is an explicit commentary on the fall of the Roman Empire; Thomas Hobbes' *Leviathan* was called forth by the civil wars of seventeenth-century England; and it was the degeneration of the *ancien régime,* as manifest in the artificiality and loneliness of Parisian intellectual life and the autocracy of royal officials, that inspired the essays of Rousseau. Hence, we must begin our questioning with an effort to probe the grounds of estrangement: the extent to which it is rooted in man's nature; and by what means, and how far, it can be overcome.

The most fundamental question about estrangement concerns its ultimate origin. Are such conditions as loneliness and conflict due to the very nature of man, so that as long as the human species endures men will be estranged from one another? Or is estrangement due to circumstances that can be altered, or to human characteristics that can be eliminated without destroying anything essentially human?

1. Are men estranged in essence?

Today this question presses on us from various sides, although often we do not recognize it. For example, can we hope finally to achieve harmony and understanding among all the peoples of the world? If men are not estranged in essence, perhaps we can. However, if they are thus estranged – if, for example, man has ineradicable aggressive impulses and thus cannot realize himself without combat – the aim of wise statesmanship will not be anything so far-reaching as global understanding and unity. We will be doing well if, without trying to become at one with other peoples, we can keep from hating them; it will be an accomplishment, even though wars continue to occur, if fighting is confined to limited areas and to the less destructive weapons.

The importance of this question is exemplified also in the conflict of races. Can we hope ever to achieve full racial integration? If racial hostility is not an expression of the human essence, the ideal of full unity among the races may be reasonable. But perhaps man is essentially a suspicious and uneasy creature, readily "put off" even by superficial differences in other men. If so, even if racial differences are trivial and nonessential, a sensible political leader will not aim at integration among the races; absence of conflict, uniform justice, and decent conditions of life for everyone would be high ideals. As Fascism shows, it is possible to envision man in a way that invalidates even the goal of reducing conflict, and war and racial imperialism become the highest ideals.

The question of whether men are essentially estranged also presses on us through the alienation pervading contemporary middle-class life. A great many people today feel that although their lives are superficially harmonious and comfortable, they lack relationships that are substantial and significant. But could it be that what these alienated people lack is not community but full and creative individuality? Should they learn to cherish solitude rather than merely endure it when it cannot be avoided? Is the private life they find confining in actuality one of the greatest goods that can be wrested from an inevitably alien world? Such questions can be answered only by determining whether men are estranged in essence.

There are always more than two opposite answers to fundamental questions. However, in order to delineate sharply and briefly the issues presented, it will sometimes be convenient to discuss only two polar positions. This procedure will be followed in connection with the present question.

No other philosopher has so ably and pungently argued that men are essentially estranged as Thomas Hobbes (1588–1679). The natural condition of man, so Hobbes argued, is one of war "of every man, against every man." If there is no strong central government "to over-awe them all," then "men have no pleasure, but on the contrary a great deal of grief, in keeping company." Life in such a state must be "solitary, poor, nasty, brutish, and short." [1]

There are, so to speak, two levels of estrangement in Hobbes' philosophy. One level is psychological. Men are estranged simply because they are essentially egotistical. Each is concerned above all with the preservation of his own life; secondarily he seeks such things as wealth and prestige. None of these can be assured without power; thus, Hobbes attributes to man "a perpetual and restless desire of power after power, that ceaseth

[1] Thomas Hobbes, *Leviathan, or the Matter, Forme and Power of a Commonwealth Ecclesiastical and Civil,* ed. with an introduction by Michael Oakeshott (Oxford: Basil Blackwell, n.d.), pp. 81–82.

only in death."[2] A man cares nothing about others except as they can help or hinder him in reaching these goals. To be this way is not at all perverse; it is man's true nature. Nor is it avoidable. Simply to be a human being is to care more about one's own life and power than about anything else.

Beneath the psychological level is what can be called the "ontological" level of estrangement. Ontology is the science of being in general, and the word "ontological" is intended here to refer to Hobbes' conception of the nature of being. Hobbes is ordinarily, and accurately, considered a materialist. What this means, in Hobbes' case, is that every reality is wholly definable in terms of space, time, and laws of causation. The universe is composed of objects in motion; every reality has a definite location in space and time and is governed by invariable physical laws. A human being is simply one of the objects making up the universe; he is more complex than such things as rocks and trees, but not essentially different. What concerns us at this point is only one consequence of this view, namely, that unity among human beings, as we usually understand it, is impossible. Material objects are essentially external to one another; they cannot be united by such bonds as compassion, empathy, or a common purpose. They can be united only in the sense of being put in the same place or forcibly joined together, as in building a wall with stones. For Hobbes men are material objects and he logically concluded that they could be united only by the power of an absolute government.

Many thinkers have argued that men are essentially united. Probably the most influential of these is Aristotle (384–322 B.C.), who expressed the ancient Greek feeling for the primary and all-pervasive reality of the city-state. For Aristotle, just as a leaf in its innermost nature is part of a tree, man is thoroughly and inescapably a member of a city. "The man who is isolated – who is unable to share in the benefits of political association, or has

[2] *Ibid.*, p. 64.

no need to share because he is already self-sufficient – is no part of the polis [the city-state], and must therefore be either a beast or a god." [3] Aristotle did not carry the concept of unity to its logical extreme, which would be the ideal of a global and egalitarian society. Men could not unite on any wider scale, Aristotle believed, than that of the city-state; moreover, even within the city-state only a few could attain the full unity of common citizenship, most people being fitted only to be artisans, laborers, or even slaves. Despite these qualifications, however, Aristotle's political thought is a sober and powerful denial that men are essentially estranged. Perhaps his most famous utterance is that "man is a political being" – a being who cannot realize his essence in solitude and privacy but only in the company of fellow citizens.

But if, as Aristotle argued, men are not estranged by virtue of human nature, how does it happen that throughout history peace and harmony have been so temporary and elusive?

2. If men are not estranged in essence, how are the divisions and conflicts among them to be explained?

This question presents a simple (although not easily resolved) issue: if men are not estranged in essence, the divisions and conflicts among them must be due either to man himself or to circumstances external to man. Let us consider first the former alternative – that man causes estrangement even though he is not in essence estranged from his fellow men.

What could this mean? How could it be said that men cause estrangement but are not essentially estranged? The answer is delineated as sharply as anywhere in the thought of Saint Augustine (354–430). For Augustine, God did not intend man to

[3] Aristotle, *Politics,* translated by Ernest Barker (Oxford: Clarendon Press, 1946), p. 6.

live in a state of division and conflict, and, hence, it is not due to the human essence, which was created by God, that man finds himself in such a state. What has happened is that man has betrayed his essence. This betrayal is what Augustine and other Christians mean by "sin." Man has carried out a tragic rebellion against the order of God's creation. In doing this he has rejected his nature as received from God and has become in actuality something other than what he is in essence. The unity of divine creation has been lost. Neither God nor the human essence created by God can be blamed for this dreadful derangement, but only man in his perversity.

To understand sin as Augustine envisioned it, however, it is crucial to realize that sin is not merely a tendency of the will; it is a settled and – humanly – unchangeable configuration of the will. Man not only commits particular wrongs; he does so out of a confirmed disorientation of soul. But he is still responsible – not only for the particular wrongs he commits but for the state of will from which they arise. It is this primal responsibility that is symbolized by the concept of "original sin." Man finds himself an alien within creation, divided from both Creator and fellow creatures. So far as man's own powers go, this condition is irreparable; yet it is one's own fault. There is hope only in the grace of God. Many people today are bored or repelled by this kind of dark and censorious theology. It must be recognized, nevertheless, that Augustine described a strange but common experience: many men feel unable to resist doing things for which they nevertheless condemn themselves.

Augustine's is a fearful and impressive philosophy, with its picture of men as a ruined race toiling in a world where there is no light aside from the gleams of God's mercy. Equally powerful philosophies, however, have been founded on the idea of human innocence. This idea is old because, besides being possibly true, it is pleasant. Augustine devoted much time and effort to attacking Pelagius, a monk who argued that man has it within his own power to turn away from sin. But perhaps the most eloquent claims to human innocence are found in modern times in the writings of Jean Jacques Rousseau (1712–1778).

If men are essentially united and have never betrayed their essence, how has their history come to be filled with so much hatred and turmoil? The only possible answer is that men have in some way accidentally (due to no grave, inherent defects of nature) become entangled in circumstances that have estranged them from one another. Rousseau's conviction was that a misfortune of this kind had occurred far back in history. His faith in man did not lead him to palliate the evils of human society; on the contrary, he was one of the most bitter and radical social critics of modern times. But he did not blame the dislocations of society on man – not on his essence and not on any deliberate and irreversible repudiation of his essence. Early in man's career on earth, property and power came to be concentrated in the hands of a few. This did not happen because men were extremely evil, but it subverted the natural decency of men and the natural harmony of human relations. The ensuing loneliness and discord, however, are not irremediable; they can be overcome by the good will which man has always had and which he retains despite the conditions history forces on him.

The Augustinian and Rousseauean views of estrangement have powerful reverberations in other spheres of political thought. For example, conceptions of the value and function of established institutions are largely determined by the alternative that is chosen. According to the Augustinian philosophy, man is a dangerous being; existing social and political institutions may be imperfect, but so far as they assure some kind of order, even if only through the pressures of habit and fear, they have definite value. From the Rousseauean standpoint, however, mere order is worth very little, for man is capable of realizing far greater values than order; he can attain justice and happiness. Rousseau saw the institutions of his time as keeping men from being, not Augustinian malefactors but Aristotelian fellow-citizens. This is not to say that Augustine always, and Rousseau never, approved of established institutions. For Augustine institutions are made by sinful men and are bound to have much evil in them; Rousseau thought that the original virtue of man's will had occasionally, as in the ancient Roman Republic, escaped corruption and gained sovereign power in a society. But for Augustine, heaven on earth is impossible and any order of life precluding the hell on earth that is implicit in man's nature deserves some appreciation. Rousseau, however, considered perfect order implicit in man's nature; any order that is very imperfect is intolerable degradation.

This suggests another aspect of the issue. An Augustinian, viewing man as evil and dangerous, can hardly help being nervous when men undertake political action. He is almost bound to be conservative – not necessarily in the sense of revering the prevailing order but in the sense of fearing any effort to change it. But a follower of Rousseau is likely to be revolutionary. There is no reason to fear primal human impulses. Man's innocence is a capacity for historical reconstruction. As it happens, Rousseau himself was not so carefree about revolution, but the explosive effect of his thought in history was due primarily to the revolutionary implications of his psychology – implications which Rousseau had drawn out cautiously, but his posterity exuberantly.

Today in America, many students and many black people have adopted a revolutionary attitude toward the established order. There is certainly enough evil in that order, such as poverty and racial injustice, to warrant such an attitude. But is there enough goodness in man to warrant it? If it should be that Augustine is nearer the truth than Rousseau, the intolerant self-righteousness of some of the students and blacks may be the beginning of greater evils than those they attack.

We have now considered the origin of estrangement – whether it is in man's essence, in a tragic rejection of his essence, or merely in accidental historical circumstances. This puts us in a position to ask how estrangement can be overcome, or, if men are estranged in essence, how the divisions and conflicts among them can be moderated.

3. Through what human faculties can men be brought together?

"Come, let us reason together," is an injunction from Isaiah, from the Hebraic tradition, and perhaps the central idea in the minds of the ancient Greeks, so different in many ways from the Hebrews, was that men might bridge their divisions and still their conflicts through reason. Since ancient times, countless writers and leaders have called on men, for the sake of harmony, to control their passions. There is no doubt about the consensus of the West as to the faculty by which discord can be moderated or overcome; it is reason.

The role conceived for reason, however, varies in accordance with the attitudes toward estrangement that we have discussed. If men are envisioned as essentially estranged and their interests altogether in conflict, then, of course, there is little that reason can do. Far from drawing men together, it must enable the most cunning and ruthless of them to gain the advantage over others. No great political thinker (not even Machiavelli) has defended this position. But according to Plato, at least two well-known intellectual figures of his own time – Thrasymachus and Callicles – did so. For these two men, as Plato depicts them, reason was a dissolvent of the customs and superstitions that sometimes lure superior men into subordinating their own interests to the interests of others.

If there is some point at which individual interests happen to coincide, however, even though men are essentially estranged and care nothing about one another except as means and obstacles to individual satisfaction, reason might draw men together by revealing the coincidence of their interests. Such an idea underlies one of the most enduring notions in Western political thought, namely, that government is based on a "social contract." This is illustrated by the views of Hobbes. As already shown, Hobbes regarded men as estranged in essence. Yet he did believe that all men have an interest in peace and, thus, in effective central government. Reason, he thought, could make this congruence of individual interests indisputably clear and thus could save men from the "war of all against all" into which they would otherwise fall due to their essential estrangement. For Hobbes, each man is concerned only for his own safety; but reason shows him that to reach that end he must enter into a contract to obey a government which secures the safety of all.

The Western faith in reason is at its height where essential estrangement is denied. The idea that through reason we can discern our common essence and from this source draw the laws that unite us without violating the nature of anyone is among the oldest and most durable principles of our heritage. It was the first principle of Plato's political philosophy, an elitist, city-state philosophy; in Stoicism it became the basis of an egalitarian and universalist outlook; in the Middle Ages it retained its authority, although combined with the principles of orthodox Christianity; in modern times it has been the theoretical foundation both of the idea of international law (limiting state power in its external application) and of constitutional government (limiting state power in its internal application). By using our reason, according to this view, we become members of a community that is not destroyed by the divisions and conflicts among classes and among nations. Our common membership in this universal society of reason enables us to set over all power, in its ceaseless tendency to become brutal and limitless, standards that are rationally certain and morally unchallengeable. If there is any single indispensable idea in our past it is this one.

Nevertheless, several thinkers have viewed the idea either with reservations or with definite hostility. An indication of the power of the idea is that probably no one has repudiated it altogether. But one thinker who came near to doing so, and thus serves as a convenient example of the antirationalist position, is Edmund Burke (1729–1797). Burke candidly defended prejudice in place of reason. His writings show a belief in the essential unity of men that is as emphatic and as unqualified as Aristotle's. But Burke did not trust reason accurately to disclose the human essence. He trusted instead the customs and traditions which, enthroned in the human mind, are "prejudice." Man is far too deep and complicated to be encompassed by reason; and he is too dangerous (Burke having an Augustinian view of man) to be left to the guidance of reason. In an old and awesome set of institutions like those Burke was acquainted with in England, the essence – and thus also the unity – of men is realized. But the claim to understand man by reason Burke considered as groundless pride; the result of this claim is to imperil the mutual understanding and respect that are reached through humble acceptance of established ways.

The aim of this book is to define some of the main paths of thought but not every possible path. There is no intention of suggesting that there are only a few principal routes that one who thinks can logically follow. Thought is (and should be) ingenious in finding untraveled ways. Nevertheless, the terrain of thought does impose certain common directions on those who start from the same basic principles. Accordingly, what has to be noted here is that the division between the rationalist and the Burkean positions tends to define two basically different ways of looking at the social and political world. The following polarities, in their typical forms, derive from this issue.

1. *Moral absolutism* versus *moral relativism.* Moral absolutism is the theory that there are moral standards independent both of the interests of the individual and of the standards that happen to prevail in society. The main form of moral absolutism in Western history is the idea of natural law, according to which there is a universal and eternal law based on the essence of man and discernible by reason. Plainly this idea expresses the conviction that reason does draw men together. Relativism has various

forms (depending on what morality is held to be determined by and thus to be relative to), but one of its main forms is the principle that good and evil are defined by each society. Burke was not an extreme relativist, for he believed that certain standards are incumbent on men regardless of the rules of their societies. But his regard for custom and tradition led naturally to an acceptance of many of the moral variations among times and places.

2. *Uniformity* versus *organic unity.* Reason can discover only the general – that which is common to many particulars; consequently, rationalism readily gives rise to a conception of unity in which the stress is on uniformity. In contrast, thinkers like Burke are likely to be more sensitive not only to the differences among societies, which are sanctioned by moral relativism, but also to differences among individuals – differences such as those of character, talent, and vocation – which are coordinated in the organic unity of the group. A clear expression of this polarity can be seen in Aristotle's protest that Plato erased essential differences among persons in order to unite them. "It is," Aristotle complains, "as if you were to turn harmony into mere unison, or to reduce a theme to a single beat." [4]

3. *Radicalism* versus *conservatism.* To believe that we can rationally comprehend man leads to the notion that men have the capacity and the right to destroy all those ancient institutions which rest on mere prejudice and to rebuild them in accordance with rational designs. Rationalism in this way entails radicalism. Such pride, in the face of the majestic and enigmatic past, infuriated Burke. He set against it the conservatism that necessarily follows from the principle that man's essence is disclosed only through custom and tradition. The kind of order that is built by generations of prudent statesmen cannot be deliberately constructed according to the counsels of reason. If one is fortunate enough to live within such an order, all he can do – and this is his overriding duty – is to respect and to guard it.

[4] *Ibid.*, p. 51.

Are mere human faculties, however, enough to bring men together, even assuming that they are not essentially estranged? This brings us to an issue that most people today like to ignore. The spiritual atmosphere of our time seems to be one of religious doubt along with human self-confidence. Thus it is widely assumed that we neither need to use nor can use anything but human faculties in resolving our tensions and discords. On the other hand, one of the oldest and most universal convictions is that a stable and decent society can be built only on some kind of religious ground. Numberless generations, in all parts of the globe, have assumed that men can be properly related to one another only if they are properly related to the divine. Hence we must consider whether this is so, if only in order to comprehend the humanistic convictions that now generally prevail.

4. In overcoming their divisions and conflicts, are men in any way dependent on the divine?

Three general positions answering this question can be conveniently distinguished. The first is the self-confident humanism of modern man, which is often accompanied by atheism or agnosticism and by suspicion of organized religion. No historical lessons have sunk more deeply into the American mind than those normally drawn from the religious wars in Europe and the Puritan theocracy in Massachusetts. Religious faith, it seems clear, can be both divisive and despotic. This conviction has for many been reinforced by Marxist and socialist secularism. For Marx, religion was "the opium of the people," and socialists have traditionally dismissed it as "pie in the sky." The serious allegation behind such rhetoric is that religion has often made men indifferent to the worldly sufferings of others and in this way has been an enemy of community.

The ascendant ideal today is that of a purely human community. Almost all conscientious people today assume that the time has finally come, after long ages in which the majority of human beings have lived in squalor and ignorance, to meet the pressing worldly needs of everyone; our powers of organization and production make the continuance of physical want intolerable. We must now care for one another in a measure that corresponds with our powers. Most people sharing this ideal make the further assumption that its realization need not be hindered, and may even be helped, by the weakening of religious faith which has occurred during the past two or three centuries. After all, when men felt closely united with the divine, they were usually very imperfectly united with one another; often they were horrifyingly cruel to one another. Now perhaps the love and devotion once bestowed upon God can be bestowed on our fellow men.

The humanist vision of unity can be a moving one. In its light we see ourselves as inhabiting a vast, indifferent universe, and as having no company and no help except from one another. Even most of those who still believe in God seem to feel that such a vision will suffice, as religious faith declines, to undergird our common life and action.

In view of this humanist consensus, it is striking that the political thinkers of antiquity and the Middle Ages for the most part believed that unity of man with man depends on unity of man with the divine. The first great political philosophy set forth in the West, that of Plato (427–347 B.C.), exemplifies this viewpoint. If the injunction implicit in most twentieth-century social commentary is "forget about the transcendent, and concentrate on one another," the injunction implicit in *The Republic* is "know first the transcendent, then consider one another." Plato believed that beyond all the things we can see, hear, and touch there is a source from which things draw their reality and value. He called this simply "the Good" and he likened it to the sun, which makes it possible for living things both to grow and to be seen. The being and worth of a man is a reflection of the Good. It is possible to understand man and his needs only in the light shed by the Good. It follows that there can be no authentic unity among men who are separated from the Good.

For Plato, the twentieth-century notion that we should ignore ultimate realities to concentrate on building a good society would have seemed as absurd as it would seem to a scientist today to suggest that we disregard the laws of astronomy and aerodynamics to expedite the exploration of space.

Not long after the time of Plato, Stoic philosophers began to develop a far more ecumenical and egalitarian concept of unity than Plato's; more will be said about this concept further along in this book. The point that needs to be made here is that the new concept of unity still rested on religious foundations. For the Stoics, the entire universe was divine. The duties that bind men to others are imposed by the divine order they inhabit. In this sense men are united with other human beings only because they are united with the divine.

This Hellenic conception of the dependence of the social on the religious is the second general position relating to the question we are discussing (the first having been the humanistic outlook). What distinguishes it from the third position, to which we now turn, is its reliance on human initiative. It regards the divine as inert and merely available; it is man who acts. For adherents of the third position, which is that of orthodox Christianity, it is God who acts.

In basing the unity of men on unity with God, the Christian view is like the Hellenic. A man deserves to be loved by his fellow men because of a sanctity that comes from God. For Paul we (or at least all Christians) are "members one of another." But this is only because we have been created and redeemed by God. It would have been as unthinkable to Paul as to Plato that men should love one another, or even respect one another, simply for being men. The only authentic unity is, to borrow Augustine's phrase, that of "the City of God."

But the orthodox Christian idea of the relation of the divine and the human is very different from the typical Greek idea. The latter is determined by the notion that man, primarily through reason, can ascend to God. But for Christians the idea of ascent to God, by man's own will and power, manifested pride. The myth of original sin premised human helplessness. The only possible relationship between God and man would be one established by God. Thus the notion of human ascent was replaced by that of divine descent. For Christians, the decisive act of divine descent lay in the life, death, and resurrection of Jesus.

From this standpoint the conquest of human discord is envisioned very differently from the way in which it is from the Hellenic standpoint. For Plato and for the typical Stoic it was sufficient that the divine was real and that at least some men could find their way into its presence. Such spiritual exploration and discovery might lead to the founding at least of circumscribed communities, gatherings of those who are at one with each other through being at one with the divine. But for the orthodox Christian a real community cannot come about due merely to the acts of men. It is created by God. Only God can break the chains cast by original sin and enable man to turn toward the divine and toward his fellow creatures. Community originates in the action, and not merely the availability, of the divine. This is the reason why any true city is a "City of God."

Today, many people find it hard to take religious ideas of this kind very seriously. But for many centuries in the past they were taken very seriously indeed, and one would have to be exceedingly complacent to assume that it is altogether the advanced state of our own intellects that makes the deep concerns of earlier ages so incomprehensible to us.

At the very least, we should bring ourselves to ask what we mean, from a humanist perspective, when we speak of "the dignity of the individual." This is perhaps the key phrase expressing the modern idea of community: each man deserves respect, and thus fair treatment, whatever his race or faith or class. It is easy to understand why this would be so if each man were sanctified by the divine. But if the divine is nowhere in the picture, due to what qualities does each individual deserve respect? If there is no Platonic sun of being, and no God, wherein is man's dignity? What unites us?

The four questions so far asked have enabled us to consider human relations in their most general character. We have asked about both the source and the healing of estrangement. More exactly, we have asked whether men are estranged in essence, and if not how the human essence has been lost and can be restored. It would be possible at this point to conclude the chapter and to move into other areas of thought. Some of the principles discussed may become more alive, however, if we reflect on their application to the most serious divisions among men. Over the centuries, the two most profound and unbridgeable divisions seem to have been those between peoples, such as city-states and nations, and those between classes. These will be the subjects of the final two questions of this chapter.

5. Should all peoples be united in a single, global society?

The history of thought discloses two extreme and opposed responses to this question. Both are old and enduring; both appear in ancient and in modern times as well.

Greeks in the age of Plato and Aristotle believed that a political order even as large as the modern nation-state was incompatible with a fully human life. Aristotle's assertion that "man is a political being" expressed a widely shared conviction; it was commonly assumed, however, that man can live according to his political nature only where states are small. To live in a large state is to be governed from a distant imperial center, and thus to be a subject rather than a citizen. In Aristotle's vision, men are united by a universal essence; yet only a parochial state, the *polis,* can bring about realization of that essence and of the unity it implies.

The ideal of the small, personal state has echoed and reechoed in the history of modern times as thinkers have sought ways of escaping the impersonality of the giant nation-states. Rousseau reasserted the basic standard of the ancient democracies – that a state should be small enough for the citizens to meet regularly in a single assembly. Since the time of Rousseau, some of the most idealistic thinkers have felt that only by breaking up the vast states and organizations of the modern world could community be saved. Such thinkers have been so influential that the ideas of community and of small associations have become almost equivalent in many minds. From this point of view, for all mankind to fall under a single government would be a catastrophe.

Another kind of idealism, however, is not so inspired by the idea of daily, face-to-face citizenship as by the vision of all men realizing their common human identity in a global commonwealth. This vision, like the opposite one, arose in ancient times. It was developed by the Stoics after the city-states had been incorporated in empires. The *polis* is replaced, in the thought of the Stoics, by the *cosmopolis*. As stated above, in Stoic thought the universe is a divine order; this order is manifest in laws that can be known by reason; therefore, as the Stoic Emperor Marcus Aurelius said, we all are citizens of a cosmic city. Here, in contrast with the outlook of Aristotle, the principle of a universal human essence, uniting men, is developed into the ideal of a universal human community. Stoicism was the principal philosophy embraced by the most effective statesmen of universal order in Western history – the men who administered the Roman Empire and shaped the Roman law.

Christian thinkers during antiquity and the Middle Ages were if anything more universalist than the Stoics, for they envisioned mankind as united not only by natural law and political order but also by universal sinfulness and the mercy of God. The divine offer of redemption was addressed, through the prophets and Christ, to all men; and all men properly belong in the Christian Church.

The Roman ideal of a universal and eternal peace, and the

Christian ideal of one global faith, linger as a bitter longing in the twentieth century. The Roman and Christian ideals glimmer faintly in our international law, in the United Nations, and in the horror felt before the maelstrom of nationalism, fanaticism, and war in which we seem about to be engulfed. One of the most powerful restatements of the universalist outlook is found in the philosophy of Marx. Nations are held to be organizations of a doomed class; the proletariat will establish the all-encompassing unity that finally eluded both the Roman Empire and the Christian Church. But how far we are from realizing this ancient dream is indicated by the fact that Marxism has itself contributed greatly to the self-righteousness and belligerence of some nations and has become one of the ideologies setting us against one another.

But which do we really want, associations so small and personal that they might, in accordance with a suggestion of Aristotle, be bound together by friendship, or a peace so inclusive and just that in its compass all mankind is one fraternity? Is our ideal Athens or Rome? There is of course a third alternative – the nation-state system that crystallized when the universal Church disintegrated at the time of the Reformation and that still defines the general shape of our political world.

Is the nation-state just the wrong size – too large for personal relations and too small for global concord? Most people prior to the Reformation would have said that it is. And many of the most idealistic people today would agree. The nation-state is a vast, impersonal organization; the intimate, spontaneous relations of persons seem to become nothing before its demands for money, soldiers, highly educated technicians, disciplined workers, and so forth. The student's hatred of "the Establishment," the draft, and the involvement of universities in the work of the Pentagon, doubtless arises in some part from a realization of the vulnerability of personal relations before the overwhelming and omnipresent power of the national order. At the same time, however, the nation-state is far too small to guarantee global peace and thus its might is dedicated above all to war; it brings the impersonality of a global state, but not the security and peace. In universities today the nation-state has few friends.

It is surprising, then, to realize that during the past two centuries the nation-state has been one of the chief objects of human devotion. It has been exalted even by many men of intelligence and ideals. The great German philosopher, Georg W. F. Hegel (1770–1831), may serve as an example. Hegel's attitude was that a significant community must be far more powerful and more various in its composition than a small personal association can be. It must have a military and economic effectiveness and a cultural greatness that depend on considerable size. At the same time, a significant community must be distinct from other communities; it must be a particular community, subject to comparison with others and capable of testing itself in war with them, and not simply the inconceivably vast and miscellaneous collection of people we call "mankind." For Hegel both Athens and Rome were, in the progressive unfolding of humanity, early stages, now left behind; the climax of history will occur in the era of nation-states.

These took on, for Hegel, a religious grandeur. A nation-state, he argued, is of greater reality and value than any individual human being. And in one of the most notorious assertions in the literature of political thought, he stated that it is "the Divine Idea as it exists on earth." [5] Hegel has been sharply condemned for such statements. But he only said, explicitly and philosophically, what many modern nationalists have felt.

Who is correct – the Athenian citizen, the Roman-Christian universalist, or the modern nationalist? Each one felt that he spoke for the indispensable condition of unity and life.

Let us now, by means of a final question, reflect on unity among classes. Here it would not be appropriate to ask exactly the same question that we asked about unity among peoples. The

[5] Georg Wilhelm Friedrich Hegel, *The Philosophy of History,* rev. ed. (New York: Wiley, 1900), p. 39.

great issue concerning peoples is whether there should be a global society or whether every people should retain its own sovereign identity. There is no such issue with respect to classes. By its very nature a class is part of a larger unity; it would be impossible to argue that classes should be altogether separate and sovereign groups. The question concerns the *kind* of unity linking classes. Can it be real unity, that is, just and voluntary? Or must it necessarily be exploitative and thus based on force and deceit?

6. Can any real unity be achieved without abolishing classes?

Assuming unity is good, to answer "No" is to condemn totally the Western democracies. It is to say that as societies they are unjust and oppressive because they are divided into separate classes. It is to say that as governments they are essentially despotic, despite their outward forms. It is to say, finally, that the only hope for the future is in violence, for if *no* unity can be achieved without abolishing classes, and if unity is good, it follows not only that classes must be abolished but also that this can only be done through violence, since classes, in no way united, could not possibly agree to do it peacefully.

This suggests why the "No" that emerged from the research and thought of Karl Marx (1818–1883) shook Western institutions more profoundly than has any other utterance since the Reformation.

The key to Marx's attitude lay in the importance he attributed to economic circumstances. Marx held that man's ideas and feelings – in truth his whole nature – are formed by his economic situation. Simply in order to live man must become involved in a productive system; the continuous and irresistible pressure of physical needs assures that this system will powerfully mold his whole character. This may seem at first glance to be an innocuous, if sensible, view. It implies, however, that the classes –

which Marx defined economically, the main division being between those who own property and those who do not and thus must work – are composed of completely different kinds of people. Members of one class must have different ideas and different emotions than the members of another class. They cannot possibly be united in a single community.

Reverting to the concepts we have been discussing in this chapter, what this comes to is a denial (1) that there is a common human essence uniting men and (2) that there are common, impartial faculties, such as reason, by which any such essence can be discerned. (It must be acknowledged that Marx's basic philosophy is sketchy and is susceptible of various interpretations. The following, however, is a common and plausible interpretation.) First, according to Marx, a human being cannot be identified with some abstract, changeless idea of man. Rather, he *is* what he *does*. This is to say that a man's nature is defined by his work; and therefore, those who do completely different kinds of work, such as the wage-laborer and the capitalist, must be very different kinds of beings. Further, even so far as there is some very general human essence, which makes it possible to call both the laborer and the capitalist "men," and to see (as Marx did) the frightful conditions of early industrialism as violations of man's nature, there is no faculty powerful enough to define this essence accurately and bring men to respect it. As pointed out above, man's ideas and feelings both are products of his economic situation. This is true of his ideas and feelings concerning his own essence. Thus not only are workers and owners very different in nature, they have very different conceptions of themselves.

On these grounds Marx would have had to deny that unity could be achieved without abolishing classes even if he had seen no important conflict of interest dividing the classes. He held, however, that there is such a conflict. Owners are compelled by the economic system to oppress the workers. For their part the workers must destroy the owners before they can ever gain a decent life. Thus the classes are not only different, they are the two sides in a deadly war.

Therefore, any social order that claims to be a true unity of the classes is basically fraudulent. Ruling classes will always assert that the whole population is united in accepting their governance and the ideology behind it, but this is no better than an effort to disguise the despotism they impose. The liberal democracies, for Marx, were only covert dictatorships on the part of the owners. Like many students and blacks in America, Marx held that modern democracy is only a facade; it cannot be, as it purports to be, the rule of the people, because those underneath are in a state of fundamental and incurable disagreement with those over them.

While Marx denied that all classes could voluntarily join in a single community, however, he did not deny that a real community would sometime come into being. One class, that of the workers, is the seed of such a community growing within the capitalist state. It is destined finally to break through the old institutions enclosing it and to create a classless society.

Among the philosophies opposed to Marxism in the matter of class relations, two principal types can be distinguished: the conservative and the liberal.

In conservatism like that represented by Burke, class divisions are assumed to be just and necessary. Societies need ruling groups, and some men are particularly well fitted, both by innate ability and by educational and other advantages which cannot in the nature of things be enjoyed by everyone, to be members of these ruling groups. Moreover, it is assumed not only that class distinctions are justified but that the lower classes can see that they are justified. Accordingly, the conservative idea can be said to be that of unity *through* class distinctions. Class lines not only divide men but, so long as they are required by a sense of justice that all classes share, in a way they unite them.

Let us put this in terms of the central concepts of this chapter. Through loyalty to common traditions and customs, all classes participate in the "prejudice" that unites them. This prejudice discloses man's essence, on which unity is based. The human essence is realized, however, not through the unrelenting uniformity and equality envisioned by some radicals, but by the simultaneous diversity and unity of classes.

The most effective opposition to Marxism has probably come from those who hold that, while justice does not sanction the division of society into separate and unequal classes, all classes can perceive that this is so and can cooperate in reforming the social order. This is the central idea in liberalism of the kind represented by Franklin D. Roosevelt and John F. Kennedy. According to the liberal outlook, a measure of unity can be achieved without abolishing classes – at least there is hope of abolishing classes peacefully (although of course many liberals would be satisfied to moderate class differences without totally doing away with them). The classes should unite, it is held, not in accepting society but in reforming it. As in conservatism, all classes should come together in a single community, but not in one that remains what it has always been; they should unite rather in a reforming community, one that is imperfect but that can gradually perfect itself.

Two ideas we have discussed are at the core of the liberal outlook: that men are essentially at one, and that reason enables them peacefully to realize their unity. A common essence and common rational faculties are in the final analysis of greater force than the economic system. Owners may not gladly give up unfair privileges, but they can be brought, by reason and legal pressure, to do so peacefully. Marx's basic premises – that man is made by his economic situation, and that the classes are in irresolvable conflict – largely ruled out the possibility of any such understanding between owners and workers; thus Marx was a revolutionary rather than a reformer. Unity would normally have to be created by the violent destruction of the owning class. Liberalism rests on the idea that economic estrangement is not total estrangement; a common human essence dictating harmony and common rational powers making this harmony available remain underneath all class divisions. Hence the classes can unite in the task of social change.

This faith has been of tremendous historical importance. It has been professed in one way or another by most of the governing parties in the Western democracies during the present century. It has provided the main ground on which the totalitarian extremes of Fascism and Communism have been opposed. But is it a valid faith?

For most of those who are not hungry and cold, liberalism is a more *appealing* faith than is Marxism. It does not tell us that we live in a doomed society or that we are obliged to take on the discomforts and perils of revolutionary action; it regards all men with affection and hope. But is liberalism a *truer* faith than Marxism? It requires great complacency to say without hesitation that it is. We see more and more clearly how skillfully, through several decades of supposedly profound social reform, the owning classes have preserved their wealth and privileges. Under the governance of these classes cities have decayed, nature has been debauched, and the wealth of the nation has been squandered in futile and barbarous wars. At the same time, workers who have gained prosperity have become defenders of racial segregation and war. It is no longer so easy to regard men with a liberal affection and hope.

But one can hardly stand on the Marxist side, either, without serious misgivings. The most serious of these, perhaps, is occasioned by the implications of the Marxist vision of class warfare. If the classes are irreconcilable enemies, has mankind any prospect before it except despotism and terror? Marx after all presented an extremely sombre vision of man's situation. He did not succumb to despair because he shared the nineteenth-century faith in the common people and in historical progress. But such phenomena as the vulgarity of popular culture have shaken the former faith, and the whole catastrophic history of the twentieth century the latter. It is no longer as easy as it was in Marx's day to rest confidence in the common people and in progress. But if we cannot do this, then Marxism spells despair.

In concluding this chapter, it should be pointed out that all of the doubts to which this and the preceding question give rise are expressions of the simple issues set forth in the first four questions of this chapter. Although the challenge of disunity among peoples and that of disunity among classes evoke different responses, and reverberate in the form of differing issues, at the roots of both are the questions we have already asked. Let these be summarily restated. Is the hatred and violence of the twentieth century a mirror in which we see ourselves as we basically and inescapably are? That is, are men essentially estranged, and if not how have they become so divided? And if it is not true that our times disclose our essence, how can we gain and enact a deeper vision? Through what faculties? And through what powers – those of man alone?

SUGGESTED READINGS

(Titles are listed chronologically. All are available in paperback or other inexpensive editions.)

Plato. *The Symposium*
———. *The Republic,* Books I–IV
Aristotle. *Politics,* Books I–III, VII–VIII
Saint Augustine. *The City of God,* Chapters 11–14
Dante Alighieri. *On World-Government (De Monarchia)*
Saint Thomas Aquinas. *The Political Ideas of St. Thomas Aquinas.* Ed. by Dino Bigongiari. (Hafner)
Hobbes, Thomas. *Leviathan,* First Part
Rousseau, Jean Jacques. *The Social Contract*
Burke, Edmund. *Reflections on the French Revolution*
Paine, Thomas. *The Rights of Man*
Marx, Karl. *Economic and Philosophical Manuscripts*
Marx, Karl and Engels, Friedrich. *Basic Writings on Politics and Philosophy.* Ed. by Lewis Feuer. (Doubleday)
Durkheim, Emile. *Suicide*

Buber, Martin. *I and Thou*
Freud, Sigmund. *Civilization and Its Discontents*
Bergson, Henri. *The Two Sources of Morality and Religion*
Berdyaev, Nicolas. *Slavery and Freedom*
Fromm, Erich. *Escape from Freedom*
Niebuhr, Reinhold. *The Nature and Destiny of Man,* Vol. I
Dawson, Christopher. *Religion and Culture*
Marcuse, Herbert. *Eros and Civilization*

3

Inequality and Equality

It is an easy step from the subject of estrangement, which we considered in the preceding chapter, to that of inequality. This is because inequality is a kind of estrangement, and a kind that is peculiarly prevalent and powerful. In practically all times and places men have been divided by inequalities of rank, power, and wealth; the life of almost everyone is decisively affected, with respect to material decency, education, associations, and vocation by the class level at which it is carried on.

It is an easy step from the subject of estrangement to that of inequality, but it is one that carries us into the center of modern political conflicts. Much of the history of our times has been made by the rebellion against privilege and power that began with the French Revolution. Socialism and communism have both been deliberate, long-sustained assaults on inequality; the twentieth-century upheavals in Asia and Africa have been inspired by the determination that wealth and world power shall not be monopolized by white men; and the turmoil in America today is stirred primarily by a black revolt against the ancient white ascendancy and a student reaction against "the Establishment."

The logical starting point for exploring this part of the terrain of political thought is a question that parallels the first question of the preceding chapter: whether, underneath all of the inequalities incorporated in the social and political order, men are really – by nature, and not just by convention – unequal.

7. Are men unequal in essence?

Certainly men are unequal in most of their physical and psychological characteristics. They are unequal in health and intelligence and emotional balance and in so many other ways that it would be tedious to try to list them. But are such inequalities perhaps due mainly to social inequalities? For example, poor health may derive from the inadequate nutrition that results from poverty; what seems to be low intelligence may be a result of the illiteracy of a lower-class household. But while particular inequalities may have social causes, it does not seem that inequality in general can be thus explained, since marked inequalities are manifest among people who have been shaped by the same conditions. Some people who have been raised in the most propitious physical circumstances are nevertheless sickly, and some who have had every educational advantage are unintelligent. Hence, there is no escaping the fact that there are natural inequalities. The question is whether any of these ultimately matter. Are men unequal in their innermost being, or only in characteristics which are inessential and ultimately irrelevant?

Today it may seem that idealism must be on the side of equality and that there is something cynical in the idea that human beings are essentially unequal; for to say that they are essentially unequal is to say that they are unequally human. Nevertheless, some of the most exalted figures in Western intellectual history have been willing to say this. Aristotle is a good example. He envisioned mankind as a great natural hierarchy.

The main determinant of rank is the degree and kind of reason one possesses. At the summit of the hierarchy are those preeminent in their powers of general understanding, such as scientists and philosophers. Somewhat beneath them are those with the good judgment fitting them to rule; they are natural kings and aristocrats. Beneath them in order come natural citizens, who are rational enough to manage political affairs with many others of their kind, and then natural artisans and workers, who should not take part in political affairs. At the base of the hierarchy are men with only enough reason to serve others; they are slaves by nature. Aristotle defined man in terms of reason; hence, to have only enough reason to be an artisan or worker is to be deficient in humanity, and to be a slave is to be hardly a human being at all. Aristotle would have regarded as a palpable and dangerous absurdity the later Christian notion that a man who is fitted neither for science and philosophy, nor for political activity, may nevertheless stand at the summit of a hidden hierarchy determined by God's grace.

Views of this kind, maintaining the essential inequality of men, usually assume one of two main forms. For some, the superiority of the few consists in their relationship with a transcendent being – with "the Good," or with God; from this point of view men are unequal in sanctity. One of the greatest proponents of this idea was Plato. In Plato's vision a few supreme men were the true philosophers who had ascended to a knowledge of the Good. Their supremacy consisted of their link with the divine. Granted, this relationship was open only to those possessing unusual powers of reason – a worldly characteristic, not necessarily involving any relationship with the divine. But these powers could be wasted. They distinguished the man possessing them from other men only as they were employed in the task of religious ascent.

For certain other thinkers the excellence of the best men is purely worldly. It consists in such qualities as political genius, artistic mastery, and athletic prowess. Excellence does not depend on any relationship with the divine; it is entirely within the person. It might be said to consist, not in being *related* to the divine but, in *being* divine.

The writings of Friedrich Nietzsche (1844–1900) constitute an extreme and moving statement of this point of view. Nietzsche believed that one condition determined the spiritual atmosphere and the duty of serious men in his time: an awakening to the fact that there is no God. "God is dead" was his melodramatic, and now trite, assertion. The main consequence of this awakening is that it is now incumbent on man to rise out of the self-destructive humility imposed by Christianity and to affirm his full worldly being. What is the nature of this worldly being? Nietzsche characterized it as "will to power." He argued that men must now unapologetically concentrate on the enhancement of their power. This did not necessarily mean political activity and war; a great artist, Nietzsche thought, might be more powerful than a Roman emperor. But it did mean inequality. The average man is weak, and a man of power is one who has struggled with and risen above the masses. Nietzsche repeatedly, and with the utmost bitterness, attacked the idea of equality, which he saw as one of the devices by which the weak, in their pettiness and rancor, crushed human greatness. Now that "God is dead," human existence depends for its grandeur on the few who, in place of worshiping transcendent gods, can themselves become human gods. For these few to realize their powers, however, Christian and democratic equality must be abolished. Human relations must again, as in ancient times, be formed by domination and rank.

Plato and Nietzsche, both maintaining that men are in essence unequal, are among the greatest names in the history of the Western spirit. Despite such authority, however, one of the most irrepressible and potent ideas ever conceived is that all inequalities in the final analysis are insignificant and that men are essentially equal. This idea had much to do with the French Revolution, with the rise of socialism and communism, and with the twentieth-century revolutions in Russia and China; today it has helped to ignite the uprisings of the black people in America and of the nonindustrialized countries in Asia and Africa. What is the basis of such an idea?

Nietzsche was right in associating the idea of equality with faith in God. The first philosophical defenses of the idea seem to have come from the later Stoics, with their belief in the divinity of the cosmos. Men were held to be equal in that each one could apprehend the main demands of the moral law implicit in the cosmos. Thus, they were equal in their relationship to the divine. If the idea of equality was planted in the Western mind by the Stoics, it deepened its roots and grew under the care of the Christians. But here too, of course, equality was not measured by strength, or intelligence, or any other worldly characteristic. It was measured by God's creativity and mercy. Every man was formed by God and, nullifying his betrayal of his origins, every man was offered redemption. Rank, power, and wealth, and distinctions in intelligence, health, and beauty all become totally irrelevant before the glory of God's redemptive descent into the world. This transcendentalism remained in the concept of equality that helped inspire the rise of modern liberal and democratic government. John Locke (1632–1704), for example, who defended the establishment of constitutional (that is, limited) government in England and influenced the framers of the American Constitution, clearly did not believe men to be equal in their observable qualities. They were, for Locke, equal only in the rights received from God. In like fashion Thomas Jefferson (1743–1826) asserted that men were *created* equal and *endowed by their Creator* with inalienable rights. Thus, the idea of a sanctity that is received through a relationship with the divine is the basis not only of a certain conception of essential rank and inequality, as in Plato, but also of the traditional idea of equality.

Among the great political thinkers only one, Thomas Hobbes, maintained that in their purely worldly qualities men are essentially equal. However, his argument will hardly appeal to the modern liberal who desires, without believing in God, to believe in "the dignity of the individual," for in Hobbes' view men are less deserving of equal respect than of equal disdain. Our equality lies in our common subjection to human limitations and drives and, above all, in our common subjection to death. Hobbes sardonically pointed to the equalizing power of death with the observation that any man can kill any other (as Oswald, probably trying consciously to raise himself out of a state of obscurity and insignificance, killed Kennedy). Further, no one is exempt from the egotistical desire to postpone death as long as possible; this was the point at which the interests of men essentially estranged came together and prompted the organization of society. Thus, if for Stoics and Christians all worldly rank and excellence melted into insignificance before God, for Hobbes all men were equal before death.

In sum, the foundation of traditional egalitarianism is religion. Where does this leave contemporary man, who is skeptical of God, the soul, and every supposedly transcendent reality, but is convinced of "the dignity of the individual"? The typical liberal today assents to Nietzsche's declaration that men of intelligence and courage can no longer rely on God but he continues, with Christians, to exalt the common man. But is this logically possible? If we deny that there is any equalizing sanctity irradiating men from beyond the world, must we now face the fact that the average human being is, by practically all standards, very imperfect and that only a few are really excellent? One may feel compassion for the average man, but how can one revere him?

Ideas on equality and inequality have profound implications for the social order. Let us consider some of them.

8. If some men are superior in essence to others, by whom and by what marks can they be identified?

The first great issue presented by this question is whether the best men, if there are such men, can be recognized at all. It is a powerful temptation to assume that they can be, for it is humbling and exasperating to think that we are blind to excellence and are arranged in an unseen hierarchy which nullifies manifest distinctions and places the worth of everyone in question. Plato, Aristotle, and Nietzsche all provided reassurance in this matter. Although most of us cannot congratulate ourselves on our worth and eminence, at least we can know where each of us stands. But the idea that excellence consists in the sanctity emanating from the transcendent rather than observable, worldly qualities forces one to ask whether excellence can be confidently recognized. How can one be sure of another's, or even of his own, relationship with the divine? This question is likely to be particularly sharp and persistent if it is believed, as in orthodox Christianity, that man's relations with God do not come about mainly through human powers but depend on divine initiative. Who is man, that he should presume to anticipate and announce God's decrees? "Judge not, that ye be not judged." [1] The most extreme and dramatic symbol of God's nullification of human rank is the Crucifixion; the Lord of all mankind, according to this symbol, died ignominiously with two thieves on a desolate hillside.

But let this idea, which must be deeply offensive to one who is in earnest about the problem of according honor and power to those who deserve it, be set aside so that we can proceed with the question. Let it be assumed that excellence is identifiable. By whom? There is much sense in the notion that if there are superior men no one can identify them but others of like quality. To argue otherwise would imply some serious defect in the superior men, a defect manifest in their inability to recognize one another with assurance. Thus, it is clear in Plato's plan for government by philosophers (those who have ascended to the Good) that the successor to a philosopher-king must be chosen by the philosopher-king himself. And Plato was bound to take this position, since he believed unqualifiedly in the superiority of

[1] Matthew 7:1.

the philosopher to all other men. In short, the argument for a self-chosen elite, given elitist premises, is valid.

The paradoxical idea is that of an elite chosen by their inferiors, and it is a surprising fact in the history of thought that this idea is very old and has been supported by many distinguished thinkers. The main form of this idea is the principle that government is legitimate only with the consent of the governed. This principle was common both in ancient times and in the Middle Ages, long before the rise of modern democracy. It has been called forth not so much by confidence in the judgment of the people as by the moral conviction that no one can be rightfully subjected to power without his consent. But the moral conviction cannot be put into practice without some confidence in the people. Thus, a number of thinkers who believed in government by a superior few, placed enough trust in the good sense of average men to assert that the pre-eminent minority is to be identified, at least to the extent of being accepted, by the common majority.

By what marks can the superior few be identified? The most common answer out of the past is one which it is hard for most people now to take seriously. It is that the best are to be found among the well-born. This was a very widespread belief during antiquity and the Middle Ages. Even John Locke, the principal theorist of modern liberalism, undoubtedly assumed that government would generally be carried on by members of the hereditary aristocracy. That we find it very difficult today to understand how men for so long could have accepted birth as a major sign of virtue testifies to the hold democratic ideas have on our minds. But what sign is more reliable?

There are many possible answers to this question, but the main answer of the modern world has undoubtedly been success. Excellence is not indicated by one's ancestry but only by one's own performance. There are many possible kinds of success – political, military, and academic, for example – but the kind most acclaimed in recent centuries has probably been that gained in business. As is well known, many early Calvinists believed that business success was a sign even of the kind of excellence prized by God. This view has been embodied in the philosophy of economic free enterprise, where it is held that the best test of human quality is an unrestricted market, where each one is free to produce, to sell, and to buy as he sees fit. Business success would not seem to be a very reliable sign of the kind of excellence needed for ruling, but in America it has been often assumed that it is, probably due both to America's esteem for businessmen and to its lack of esteem for politicians.

Do we in the latter half of the twentieth century, however, believe any more strongly in success than we do in good birth? Many of the best educated and most intelligent young people seem exceedingly cynical about business success. Many of them may finally seek it, but few seem likely to do so with the sense that thus they test and prove their worth as human beings. As for political success, it is unlikely that the most sensitive young Americans regard that as any more trustworthy a sign of personal superiority than having made a great deal of money in advertising or stocks. In general, those who have "made it" in almost any field are likely to be vilified as members of "the Power Elite" or "the Establishment."

But if neither birth nor success is a reliable mark of excellence, by what criteria can we apportion power and honor? Many young people appear to evade this question through a kind of casual anarchism in which they assume that we do not need to apportion power and honor. But is this so? It can be argued that the shortest route to a system in which power is brutal and honors meaningless is by way of the assumption that neither power nor honors are necessary. The tyrannies in Russia and China, for example, are based on a philosophy that assumes the state must "wither away." Undoubtedly it is a kind of progress that students are no longer taken in by the pretensions of the well-born or the successful, but it leaves them facing the imposing question of how society is to be organized.

Let us consider the problem from the side of the idea of equality.

9. If men are essentially equal, are all conventional inequalities, such as wealth and status, wrong?

The idea that men are essentially equal, it is strange to say, had been a traditional tenet in the Western political mind for over a thousand years before it shaped up into a really serious attack on conventional inequalities. Neither Stoics nor Christians sought to abolish even slavery, let alone other established ranks. This was partly because they believed that nothing mattered except the condition of one's own soul and that this was not necessarily affected by one's position in the social order. It was partly also because they viewed all rank and power as sanctioned by God. The result was an attitude somewhat disrespectful yet submissive. The inequalities established by the social order were at once condemned and tolerated – condemned because they were not in accord with the principle of equality and tolerated because of their ultimate insignificance and their dependence on divine permission.

However, as soon as it came to be thought first, that the social order does affect the character and happiness of individuals, and second, that the social order is not controlled and sanctified by God, the idea of equality began to shake and destroy the hierarchies of the established order. The idea could be likened to a volcano which was dormant so long that people forgot its potency and built villages on its sides but which suddenly began to erupt and to bring earthquakes and fire on all of the human structures around it. If men, rather than God, make the social order and its ranks, if in doing this they are determining their own chances for personal dignity and happiness, and if, finally, all men are essentially equal, giving special privilege and irresponsible power to anyone becomes intolerable.

In the eruption of egalitarianism, the two principal thinkers, the volcanic figures of modern thought, were Rousseau and Marx. Both manifested a new sense that the individual's whole life and being are shaped by society, and both as well reflected the loss of faith that society is governed by God. Both were moved by the idea of equality to challenge priests, kings, aristocrats, and all other "dominations and powers" (to use a phrase of Santayana's). We live today amidst institutional ruins Rousseau and Marx did much to produce, and we hear all around us continuing reverberations of their challenges to conventional inequalities.

It is not hard to sympathize with their views. It is by no means clear that men are unequal in essence. At least it does not seem clear enough to justify the inequalities in wealth, power, and privilege that have prevailed in almost every society. It is not far-fetched to see the subjection and deprivation suffered by the masses throughout history as a kind of continuing outrage perpetrated by the "respectable" elements.

Still, people seem to be definitely unequal in important characteristics, such as intelligence and emotional balance, and it seems as though social order of any kind must entail inequalities of power and rank. Is the abolition of all conventional inequalities compatible with the elementary requirements of human organization? Both Rousseau and Marx stood for the general principle of radical democracy, government carried on either directly by the people or by representatives held closely responsible to the people. However, in drawing up governmental plans, as in his proposals for the government of Poland, Rousseau was willing to allow definite inequalities of wealth, rank, and power. The followers of Marx, of course, felt compelled to make even more far-reaching concessions of this kind, to the extent of establishing what may be regarded as a new kind of class dictatorship.

This terrain of thought will be viewed from another vantage point when questions concerning power are discussed in the following chapter. Meanwhile, our present reflections may be brought to a close by considering a question which brings together the subjects of these first two chapters, unity and equality. We pointed out at the beginning of this chapter that inequality is one of the most important forms of estrangement. This suggests that estrangement might be conquered by doing away with inequality. Is this true?

10. If all conventional inequalities are abolished, will estrangement necessarily disappear?

This is one of the central questions of the present time because it asks, in effect, how an industrial society can be humanized. Traditional radicals and reformers, such as English socialists and American liberals, found the answer in equality. The harsh distinctions between classes seemed the most inhuman thing about industrial society and radical and reformist movements have in general pushed for equalization. At the same time, however, one of the most bitter and widespread complaints in the highly industrialized societies has concerned, not class distinctions and inequities, but personal alienation. Both the rich and the poor, it has been argued, compose a "lonely crowd," and the rich are about as lonely as the poor. It is easy, and probably valid, to say that loneliness is far more bearable for the rich than for the poor. The fact remains that one of the major grievances of industrial man is not, on the face of things, identical with the inequality that radicals and reformers have taken to be the main illness of industrial society. The question is whether the estrangement suffered today is traceable to the inequality attacked by traditional radicalism. Will equalization destroy estrangement? There are two very different views on this matter, and the future of industrial civilization is bound to depend heavily on our capacity to decide correctly between them.

Both Rousseau and Marx in effect merged the problem of estrangement in that of inequality by arguing, or implying, that estrangement would disappear with the abolition of conventional inequalities, which for both were based on the concentration of property in the hands of a few. Both thinkers were acutely aware that something in modern life was weakening and severing the relationships of men to one another and to the physical world. Rousseau's *Confessions* is a poignant account of a lifetime of personal isolation; *Das Kapital* might be described as a long, detailed analysis of the fragmentation of life wrought by capitalism. But one of the crucial points in the social theory of both Rousseau and Marx concerns the conventional inequalities. Beneath the many estrangements men suffer is one great estrangement which causes all the rest – that between the few, who own most of the property and, thus, control the government, and the many, who own little or nothing and are the helpless subjects of an alien political power. Due to this great division, the multitudes live in circumstances which make a creative and communal existence impossible. The one thing needed to restore wholeness of life is to abolish the distance between the few and the many. By making men equal, estrangement will be overcome.

During the last century, however, there arose on the part of certain highly individual, but profound and influential, thinkers the very opposite notion, namely, that by making men equal, estrangement is deepened. One of the earliest and greatest of these thinkers was the Danish religious philosopher, Søren Kierkegaard (1813–1855). The kind of estrangement that mattered most to Kierkegaard was estrangement from God. This he thought was likely to be reinforced by equality. His argument, like that of most thinkers of his type, was directed against "mass society" or society of the sort in which everyone is at least outwardly about the same and uniqueness is censured and suppressed. Kierkegaard's short essay *The Present Age* was an attack on conformity written long before such attacks became fashionable and in themselves examples of conformity. Kierkegaard was disturbed by the disappearance, as he saw it, of individuals, of people capable of passion and decision. Only individuals can be Christians, for authentic Christianity depends on a decisiveness that sets one apart from all others. To be a Christian because everyone is a Christian is, in truth, not to be a Christian at all. Thus for Kierkegaard the leveling which seemed to be occurring everywhere around him and which meant that everyone became merely a passive reflection of everyone else was a stifling of Christianity. In this sense, equality is estrangement from God.

Other thinkers in whom the weakening of the conventional inequalities inspired doubt or fear, rather than expectations of human reunion, were in some ways quite different from Kierkegaard and from one another. Alexis de Tocqueville (1805–1859) was an aristocratic student of modern democratic institutions and attitudes whose style as a writer, in contrast with Kierkegaard's confessional ardor, was one of cool penetration. Nietzsche, as already brought out, was an atheist, sharing Kierkegaard's passionate state of mind but not his outlook. In the twentieth century, José Ortega y Gasset (1883–1955) was a cultivated Spanish philosopher who manifested little of Kierkegaard's faith, Tocqueville's interest in political institutions, or Nietzsche's hatred of Christianity, but in the spirit of all of them denounced "the revolt of the masses." These thinkers, with all of their idiosyncrasies, were united in the conviction that the rise of equality presses the individual into conformity with "the crowd" and thus alienates him from his own real nature. But a man who is alienated from himself cannot help but be alienated from others, even though he may in appearance be just like them. Thus, ironically, as equality is attained, unity is lost.

This is not necessarily a conservative outlook. The critics of mass society have not generally made a central issue out of the preservation of traditional institutions or aristocratic rank. But all of them have refused to accept the common radical principle that the abolition of special privileges and power is the way to social integration.

In what direction, then, should we move today? Even radicals find it difficult to deny that estrangement has become profound in the industrial societies, but they do deny that any real equalization has occurred. On the other side, some conservatives assert that the social and political history of the last two centuries has been one of drastic equalization and that this is what has made the present an age of individual displacement and anguish. It will be apparent to the reader, further, that these are not the only possible viewpoints. For example, equality could be necessary for unity but an inhumane and alienating kind of equality may destroy unity. Marx suggested that this is so in a warning against a kind of communism in which "the role of *worker* is not abolished, but is extended to all men." [2] And on the other side, of course, a proponent of inequality could argue that human unity depends on a particular kind of hierarchy, not simply any kind that is sanctioned by tradition, and that the task of the present is to establish new "dominations and powers." All that seems certain is that the alternatives are numerous and confusing but the anguish of our time commands us to think and to choose.

SUGGESTED READINGS

(*Titles are listed chronologically. All are available in paperback or other inexpensive editions.*)

Plato. *The Republic*
Aristotle. *Politics*, Books I and III–VI
Locke, John. *The Second Treatise of Government*
Rousseau, Jean Jacques. *Discourse on the Origin of Inequality*
Paine, Thomas. *The Rights of Man*
Tocqueville, Alexis de. *Democracy in America*, 2 vols.
Kierkegaard, Søren. *The Present Age*
Marx, Karl. *Capital*, Vol. I
Marx, Karl, and Engels, Friedrich. *Basic Writings on Politics and Philosophy*. Ed. by Lewis Feuer. (Doubleday)
Nietzsche, Friedrich. *Thus Spake Zarathustra*
Le Bon, Gustave. *The Crowd: A Study of the Popular Mind*
Ortega y Gasset, José. *The Revolt of the Masses*

[2] Karl Marx, *Economic and Philosophical Manuscripts*, trans. by T. B. Bottomore, in Erich Fromm, *Marx's Concept of Man* (New York: Frederick Ungar, 1961), pp. 124–125. The italics are Marx's.

4

Power

The discussion of unity and disunity, and of equality and inequality, brings us to an advantageous position from which to begin exploring what may be taken as the main subject of political science and thought, power. Because men are disunited, power seems necessary for assuring order. Because men are unequal, power seems justified as a way in which the virtues of the few can be useful to all. Further, many of the controversies of politics have to do with the impact of power in separating men (as in racial segregation) or uniting them (as in racial integration), in ranking them (as in allowing special tax benefits to certain classes of businessmen) or in equalizing them (as in guaranteeing a minimal annual income). Given these interconnections, the preceding two chapters have prepared us for reflecting on power.

Some of the most basic and difficult questions about power arise from its moral dubiousness. Perhaps power is essentially evil. At any rate, the use of power normally involves much evil, such as its tendency to make those who possess it arrogant and, further, the use of power presupposes evil, such as the conflicts which render order dependent on power. That human relations are pervaded by power is one of the most unmistakable signs of the radical imperfection of man.

But is man radically imperfect? Is power absolutely indispensable? Some of the greatest and most idealistic men, the Russian novelist Leo Tolstoy, for example, have answered both questions in the negative and have called for the drastic curtailment, or even the total elimination, of power. If politics is the use of power, clearly one of the first questions of political thought is whether power really is necessary.

11. Can there be any order, among men, aside from that created and sustained with power?

The argument that there can be has been based, in the political thinking of the past, on at least three different ideas. One of these is that men are good and order is, consequently, spontaneous. John Locke, for example, in framing the philosophy of liberal government, assumed that men are fundamentally reasonable. This meant, for Locke, that most people have the sense to see that others, simply because they are human beings, have certain rights, such as the right to life. It meant also that most people are disposed to respect these rights. Locke saw men as having both the capacity and the inclination to live according to the laws of nature. As a result, they need power only for overcoming certain deficiencies in the order men spontaneously keep. They do not need it for creating order.

Another principle on the basis of which it has been argued that order is not wholly dependent on power is that of natural harmony. Probably the clearest illustration of this view is the theory of the classical economists, a school of thought that flourished in the nineteenth century and provided what is still the basic outlook of most supporters of capitalism, or "free enterprise." The classical economists did not regard men as good. On the contrary, they assumed that they were generally materialistic and self-seeking. But from this they did not conclude that order must be created and sustained with power. They believed that if governments would merely assure the main conditions of individual economic activity, such as security of property and stability of currency, but otherwise would not curb the freedom of men to seek profits in accordance with their own selfish promptings, good order would come into being naturally. The products most needed by society would be manufactured voluntarily. Those making such products would be justly rewarded by the purchasers. Those making nothing, and thus contributing nothing to society, would sell nothing and in this way be automatically penalized. All of this would ensue from natural economic laws. For the classical economists, order depended not on power but on the "invisible hand" (Adam Smith's phrase) of the free market.

Finally, many thinkers have seen order as depending primarily on habit, custom, and tradition. They have not had to assume either human goodness or natural harmony. They have held, rather, that over the generations people spontaneously develop an order of life which is supported both out of habit and out of respect for ancient ways. Order rests on the human tendency to do what has always been done and to think what has always been thought. Obviously, if the principle of human goodness is radical, since it leads naturally to a willingness to abandon established arrangements and restraints, the principle that order arises from habit and from loyalty to tradition is conservative.

Anarchism is the idea that one of these forces – human goodness, natural harmony, or custom and tradition – or a combination of them, suffices to assure order and that government, therefore, can be abolished. In particular, anarchists count on human goodness because the other forces creating order – those effecting some natural harmony and those inherent in custom and tradition – contain an element of coercion. One who acts under the sway of natural forces or of habit is not fully free. Typical anarchism is the idea that goodness can replace power.

A far more common position is that a measure of order can be achieved through some combination of these forces but that they have to be supplemented with deliberate human power. This idea underlies modern liberal government. It assumes that men are decent although not perfect, that the laws of supply and demand will harmonize some relationships but not the entire society, and that custom and tradition contribute to social integration but do not alone assure it. The conclusion follows that government is not the sole source of order – and, thus, the scope of governmental power can and must be limited – but that government still is necessary.

At the opposite pole from anarchism and liberalism is the view that man is irremediably disorderly. Every source of order, aside from power, is more or less ineffective. This view was common among early churchmen and theologians, with their emphasis on original sin. It was held by Hobbes as a logical result of the idea that men are essentially estranged. Its most notorious representative is Niccolo Machiavelli (1469–1527). Contrary to his lurid reputation, Machiavelli probably had a somewhat less cynical view of man than either Augustine or Hobbes. He wrote often of the virtue and the corruption of peoples. In Machiavelli's mind, virtue consisted of qualities such as loyalty and honesty that make it possible for a people to keep order without being forced to, whereas corruption required the absolute rule of princes. Nevertheless, Machiavelli regarded all uncoerced and uncontrived order as highly unstable, and this was the heart of "Machiavellism." Human beings tend always to be fickle and selfish. They are ingenious and tireless sources of chaos. Hence, order depends on the resolution and skill of political leaders. Machiavelli's two main works, *The Prince* and the *Discourses*, both consist wholly of reflections on the techniques and devices of political and military art. If there is a central teaching in Machiavelli, it is the concept implicit in his pessimistic appraisal of man: that order, and hence civilization, rests not on human goodness but on the political sagacity of rulers.

The issue marked out by anarchism and liberalism on one side and by Machiavellism on the other is forced on us today by the disorder in the world and in American society. The hatred and confusion filling Africa, Asia, and Latin America, the revolt of American blacks against white domination, and the disruptive acts of radical students, all make it clear that order cannot be taken for granted. Does order among nations today depend on the incomprehensibly destructive and expensive armed forces of the United States? Does order within the United States require that police be freed from procedural rules that protect individuals from unfair treatment but may inhibit the suppression of crime?

As these questions indicate, in asking whether there can be any order aside from that created and sustained with power, one is asking to what degree life can be free and cooperative. This is a basic and difficult question. Still, it is only one of several such questions that are put before us by the fact of power. To begin with, as soon as it is concluded that power cannot be eliminated from human associations the question arises as to its moral effect on those who wield it. Does it enable them to be benefactors? Does it inevitably corrupt them?

12. Is it good to possess and use power?

Two diametrically opposed answers, which come to us from antiquity, can serve to dramatize the issue. For Aristotle, politics, that is, the possession and use of state power, constituted a particularly favorable sphere for the realization of one's humanity. When Aristotle said that "man is a political being," he meant in part that through political activity man realizes his full human potentialities. Man's essential unity with other men is affirmed only through entering into political life. This is to say that man's essence, as expressed in virtues like courage, pride, and truthfulness, can be realized only through the amplitude of opportunities for action that accompanies the possession and use of power.

Aristotle's conviction has been shared by many public figures. High offices, carrying great powers, have seemed to be places where a man could cultivate his imagination, demonstrate his virtues, and act on his ideals. For example, it has often been argued that the American presidency enhances the stature of its occupant. Private life, by contrast, is looked upon as constricting and demeaning.

Another great thinker of antiquity, however, took a completely different position. The viewpoint of Epicurus (342?–270 B.C.) was summed up in the injunction "Live unknown." The great problem Epicurus was trying to deal with was the general disorientation of life, not unlike the "alienation" of the present, that was suffered with the passing of the city-state as a viable life-form. Epicurus, with a number of other philosophers, tried to discover how the individual, living in a world that suddenly seemed vast and strange, could carry on an untroubled and self-sufficient existence. This search led him to repudiate the notion that "man is a political being." Politics means the very opposite of a good life. It means continuous vexation, dependence on others. Only in private life – a kind of tomb for an Aristotelian – can there be serenity and independence. Thus, today an Epicurean observer of American life might well say that a man is a fool to seek, as many do, the continual anguish that goes with the responsibilities of the American presidency. But a true Epicurean would condemn equally the campus militants who, without holding office, try to influence political affairs. The politics of protest, no less than that of high office, violates the rule of detachment.

Aristotle and Epicurus define either end of a wide range of possible answers to the question of whether it is good to possess and use power. Probably most Americans today would say that it is not good in the sense of bringing fulfillment and happiness but that it is good in the sense of being a duty. This position was developed by the Stoics a century or more after the time of

Epicurus, and it contributed to the kind of political resolution that was needed to administer and defend the Roman Empire. For the Stoics, the idea that the entire universe is a divine order dictated the determined performance of the duties of whatever station one found himself placed in by Providence. Thus political office should not be sought. If one is a slave, he should accept that lot and realize that his humanity depends on *how* he occupies his station and not on *what* the station is. But if one faces political tasks, then he should do them regardless of the uncertainties and discouragements (for example, what should be done? how can one man accomplish anything?) that are apt to assail a conscientious person in a position of power. Whatever the truth of this outlook, one has to admit that it is apt to be useful in times of trouble. Rome found it so, and perhaps America will too.

But note should be taken also of a less wholesome outlook which, in disturbed times, is bound to gain adherents. Power may not be morally or socially beneficial, according to this outlook, but it is eminently worth having, either for the opportunity it gives to a ruthless and unsentimental man to satisfy his own interests, or just for the pleasure and exhilaration of wielding it. One does not expect to find such an attitude argued by philosophers so much as merely assumed by the opportunists infesting public life. What is perhaps its sole appearance in the writings of a great thinker is by no means blatant. There is conclusive evidence that Machiavelli was not indifferent either to the ends sought by men of power or to the inherent morality of the means they employed. Success was not everything for Machiavelli. He was, however, deeply fascinated with power, so much so that he often envinced satisfaction with an adroit political maneuver and showed relatively little concern either with its ultimate consequences or its inherent morality. Moreover, the charm of power seems to have been enhanced, in Machiavelli's eyes, when it assumed some of its more violent and terrifying forms. Thus, while we cannot say that Machiavelli explicitly defended the idea of power for its own sake, his writings do sometimes express the feeling that power is in some measure justified simply by the glory and excitement of political virtuosity.

Now let it be assumed that, reflecting on the first two questions of this chapter, one has become convinced both of the practical necessity of power and of the moral legitimacy of wielding it. What about those underneath? Why should one submit to the power of others?

13. Why obey?

To possess power has at least a superficial dignity. To be without power, however, and subject to the power of another, is, at least superficially, degrading. Why should one accept such a position? This is one of the central questions in the whole history of political thought, for if it cannot be answered then the entire political order, with all of its offices, laws, and dignities, is indefensible.

Undoubtedly the oldest and most durable answer to the question is one which today seems absurd, the divine right of kings. Until three or four centuries ago most governments claimed that their power was given to them by God. And this has been true not only of Christian societies. "From the beginning of history," writes the historian Christopher Dawson, "the king has been distinguished from the tyrant, the magistrate or the official by the possession of a *charisma* or divine mandate which sets him apart from other men." [1] One of the main inferences drawn from this principle was of course the rule of absolute obedience. Political resistance is rebellion against the divine.

The concept of the divine right of kings, however, does not seem so much an answer to the question "Why obey?" as an effort to stifle the question itself. The concept is thoroughly irrational, not primarily because it is based on a religious premise, but because from the premise – that God is – the conclusion does not

[1] Christopher Dawson, *Religion and Culture* (New York: Meridian Books, 1948), p. 109.

follow. The idea that God has sanctified every government is no more necessitated by religious faith than is the idea that He has sanctified every revolution. Thus it seems reasonable to regard the idea that kings rule by a divine right not as a result reached by open-minded thinkers but as an emotion indulged in order to suppress an explosive question.

What seems a complete change of mind has, of course, occurred during recent centuries. Worldliness and religious skepticism have rendered the divine right principle wholly implausible, and the idea of personal freedom has necessarily made people question the duty of obedience in matters of serious moment to the individual. At the same time, the rising self-confidence and political awareness of the multitudes of ordinary people have given disobedience revolutionary, history-making potentialities. Thus the question of obedience has been stated with mounting insistence and portentousness. Today in America, for many conscientious and intelligent people, such as those working for civil rights and peace, the presumption that government is to be respected and obeyed has disappeared almost completely, and disobedience has taken on the aura of a virtue.

The simplest defense of obedience is undoubtedly that contained in the idea of consent. As Locke put it, "Men being . . . by Nature, all free, equal and independent, no one can be put out of this Estate, and subjected to the Political Power of another, without his own *Consent*."[2] Thus, one is not obliged to obey unless he has voluntarily agreed to do so. At one point, at least, Locke seems to imply that not only does the founding of a government require consent but that every governmental command affecting significantly one's life or rights requires a separate act of consent, for he writes that "the *Supream Power cannot take* from any Man any part of his *Property* without his own consent."[3] If this injunction were literally interpreted, payment of

[2] John Locke, *Two Treatises of Government*, ed. by Peter Laslett (Cambridge: University Press, 1960), p. 348. The italics are Locke's.
[3] *Ibid.*, p. 378. The italics are Locke's.

taxes would be voluntary. And of course to say that a man is under no obligation to obey unless he consents to do so in that particular case is to say that he is under no obligation to obey at all.

The Lockean answer to the question of political obligation represents a drastic subordination of government to freedom. Nothing can be demanded of an individual except that which accords with his uncoerced and fully conscious will. It is not surprising that some political thinkers have sought to formulate a doctrine of obedience with less anarchistic overtones. The result is as clearly represented as anywhere in the theory of the general will, which was definitively formulated by Rousseau, although it had been implicit in a number of political philosophies, such as those of Plato and Aristotle.

According to this theory, the obligation to obey a government does not depend on a prior act of consent, although Rousseau added this idea to his political theory. A government deserves to be obeyed if its commands conform to the general will. What makes a will general? Not its being the will of everyone, despite Rousseau's hope that it would be, for this would make the theory of the general will only another form of the theory of consent. What makes a will general is its end, namely, the good of everyone. The will of just one person might be the general will if its object were the common good. It is not necessary here to ask whether, in any conceivable circumstances, there can be a truly common good, a value shared equally by every member of a society. This depends on whether, in answer to the first question in this book, men are essentially at one. The main point here is that according to the theory of the general will it is possible for a group of human beings to have a common good and only so far as it represents this good does government have a moral claim to be obeyed.

For understanding this theory it is essential to realize that the general will is not necessarily willed by very many. A will is general if its end is the good of all even if the one whose will it is (Plato's philosopher-king, for example) is completely alone in seeing what is needed. It is also essential to realize that one who does not discern the general will and obeys a government that does, obeys himself alone in the sense that in serving the common good he serves his own good. But this leads to the startling conclusion that in obeying the general will one is free. A man is free, presumably, when he does what he really wants to do, what a man really wants to do is to realize his own good, and he does that in obeying the general will.

The main problem presented by the question, "Why obey?" is that of reconciling obedience with liberty. "To renounce liberty," as Rousseau asserted, "is to renounce being a man." [4] But it is of the essence of government that it demands obedience and, apparently, a renunciation of liberty. How then can even the best government be anything but a fatal abridgment of the humanity of those under it? Anarchists claim that it cannot. The theories of consent and the general will, on the other hand, are both efforts to justify government by showing how one can obey and still be free. The principal difference between the two theories is that one conceives of freedom only in terms of the conscious will and tries to legitimize obedience by tracing it back to an act of consent, while the other conceives of freedom in terms of a will that may not be fully conscious (one wills his own welfare, presumably, and yet may not know what conduces to that welfare) and thus holds that a government to which one has not explicitly consented may yet command what contributes to the individual's real good and thus enhance his freedom.

Both theories have serious difficulties. The theory of consent is simple and comprehensible on the surface, but it is very hard to see how it could be put into practice. It cannot mean that the legitimacy of every governmental command depends on a separate act of consent, for this would be incompatible with stable, effective government. Thus, it must mean that one is obliged to obey governmental commands that follow from some prior act

[4] Jean Jacques Rousseau, *The Social Contract* and *Discourses,* translated by G. D. H. Cole (New York: E. P. Dutton, 1950), p. 9.

of consent. The trouble is that rarely is a law or executive order so supported. Men are not normally related to the governments over them by acts of clear and specific consent. In reading Locke, it is easy to sense the embarrassment this difficulty causes him. In a passage concerning taxation he asserts that when property is taken from a citizen, it must be "with his own Consent, *i.e.*, the Consent of the Majority," [5] but to equate individual consent with majority consent has no manifest justification and merely presents the question of obedience in the more specific form of "Why obey the majority?" In another passage, Locke asserts that one tacitly consents to a government merely by traveling freely on its roads or even by simply being within its territory.[6] But by this standard the most despised tyrannies have rested on the consent of the governed.

And is one bound by consent which has been given due to ignorance or confusion and should not have been given? Was a young German who swore allegiance to Hitler when he first came to power in 1933 morally obliged to obey every command of the Nazi government?

On the other hand, the theory of the general will implies that one might, as stated in a notorious phrase of Rousseau's, be "forced to be free." One might be free in doing, under the eye of the police, something that he does not at all want to do. Following Hegel's assertion that what a criminal really wills is his own punishment, one might be free in prison. This is not a nonsensical idea but it is at least, in its mixing of force and freedom, a very dangerous one.

Whichever of these theories is accepted – and every theory of obedience is in some form either a theory of consent or of the general will – one is then faced with what can be called "the question of trust." If the duty of obedience must be derived from consent, what kind of government deserves consent? If it must be derived from the general will, what kind of government is likely to represent the general will?

[5] Locke, *op. cit.*, p. 380.
[6] *Ibid.*, p. 366.

14. Who should be entrusted with power?

"Anyone" and "no one" are both among the answers that have been given to this question, implausible as they may seem at first glance. The former answer is implicit in the philosophy of Thomas Hobbes. A part of the reason Hobbes thought anyone might be entrusted with power lay in his somewhat cynical egalitarianism. Hobbes had no faith in great men or aristocracies. No one was excepted from his pessimistic view of human nature. Therefore, he did not feel that it much mattered who ruled. But why did he not then assume that no one should be entrusted with power? Because he thought this would result in intolerable chaos, and because he thought that man's need for peace is so fundamental that it constitutes an identity of interest between government and people. While even the best of rulers is only a man and, thus, is thoroughly egotistical, he has the same basic goal as his subjects: a strong and well-ordered state. For the ruler this means prestige and power, for the subject security of property and long life. On these grounds Hobbes thought that any man in command of a state would be about as effective as any other and would try to further, albeit for his own advantage, the interest of his subjects.

On the other side, mistrust of power, of course, is common. But only a few relatively obscure thinkers have brought themselves to the extreme position of holding without qualification that no one should be entrusted with power. These are the anarchists. They are pessimistic in their conviction that power will always be misused. They are optimistic, however, in believing it can be dispensed with and that order and peace can be securely established without any coercion at all. Every form of power, in short, is both intolerable and useless. This may seem a strange and implausible doctrine, but it has appealed to men of great stature, such as Tolstoy, and it has a moral and logical purity that demands respect.

When we consider the answers lying in between these two extremes we cross a path which we followed in discussing the questions concerning equality in the preceding chapter. Speaking very broadly, the question as to who should be entrusted with power has been an issue fought out between the supporters of the few and the supporters of the many. The choice of sides clearly depends on views concerning inequality and equality.

Are there certain virtues, attainable by a few but not by the majority, which render those possessing them deserving of power? It has very frequently been claimed that there are. Philosophic wisdom was held by Plato to be such a virtue, the sanctity supposedly inherent in ecclesiastical ordination has been so regarded by both Catholics and Protestants, and unique practical ability has often been attributed to some minority distinguished by family background, military achievement, or business success. Indeed, human beings show a surprisingly strong inclination to exalt some minority or other. The medieval priests and kings may have been thrown down, but the twentieth century has raised up its own priestly and royal groups, as is evident in the trust that has been placed in Communist and Nazi elites as well as in scientists, technicians, and managers. The great problem has not been that people bestow their trust too sparingly, as a consideration of the defects of all elites might lead one to expect, but that they bestow it recklessly.

Today, however, many young people express total mistrust of everyone with power. Leaders in business, in government, in the churches, and in the universities have been vociferously condemned. No one should be entrusted with power, it is held, but the people themselves. This attitude has received less support in the history of political thought than one might expect. Twenty-five hundred years ago in ancient Greece, before the time of Plato, men believed in "participatory democracy," but they did not write political philosophy that has survived. Those counted among the great thinkers for the most part have treated popular government either with scorn, as did Plato, or with reservations, as did Aristotle. Only in relatively recent times has the populace been as exalted in the writings of political thinkers as have various minorities since the time of Plato and the doctrine of the philosopher-kings. Both Rousseau and Marx attributed to the people, at least in certain circumstances, something it is hardly too strong to call "sanctity." They did not regard the people as altogether subject to the corruptions that have always afflicted powerful minorities.

But is it really any more sensible to rest confidence in great numbers than in some select minority? Do the doubts most political philosophers have had about popular rule indicate a consensus of wisdom or merely that most political philosophers have in their origins and associations belonged to select minorities? The modern experience with democracy and socialism, under which the people have gained more, if not all, power, has prompted many misgivings. Numerous observers have judged the cultural tastes of the people to be vulgar and their political opinions to be based on ignorance and prejudice. But it is possible to argue that the people have not gained full power and that their failings reflect the irresponsible influence still wielded by minorities such as the overlords of press and television.

Obviously it is hard not to vacillate between the few and the many. This is why a number of thinkers, from the earliest periods of political thought, have refused to advise that either the few alone, or the many alone, be entrusted with power and have argued that the two should in some fashion share in governing. Aristotle thought this could best be accomplished through a large, powerful middle class. Rule by this class, he held, was more likely to be moderate and sensible than rule either by an aristocracy or a populace. Where a strong middle class does not exist, however, Aristotle's advice is inapplicable, for such a class cannot easily or quickly be created. Also, it is possible to feel that while neither the few nor the many should have *all* power, both have unique virtues and thus both should have *some* power. Accordingly, political thinkers have given much attention to organizational devices by which the aristocratic and democratic forms of government might be combined. It has often been argued, for example, that the executive should be reserved to those with some special distinction while the legislature should be organized to express the will of the people.

A list of the great thinkers who have urged a combination of the few and the many would include Plato, Aristotle, Cicero, Thomas Aquinas, Machiavelli, Montesquieu, Burke, and Hegel. It would be an impressive collection of names. This fact, and the arguments discussed above, suggest that there is wisdom behind the idea. An objection to it, however, that for many will seem conclusive is that there is no promise in it of the radical social and political renewal which is called for today by many students and intellectuals. It must appeal in general to those who are too satisfied, or too discouraged, to look toward the future with high expectancy. Hence for the most idealistic people today it will not answer the question of trust.

What if this question cannot be answered? If government is bound to be ineffective and corrupt, regardless of who conducts it, must we despair of man?

15. If there is no one deserving of power, how can men live with decency and dignity?

Many Christians have faced this question, particularly in the period before the Church became a ruling power. If every man is stained with "original sin," it is not to be expected that any governing power, whether a minority or a majority, will prove wise and virtuous. A deep political pessimism is inherent in the Christian outlook. It is balanced, however, by an emphatic political detachment. For an authentic Christian, to live with decency and dignity means simply to live in a way that merits salvation, and Christians have not ordinarily been willing to grant that this can in any way be influenced by governments contrary to the will of God. This view assumes that governments cannot determine anything of ultimate importance; they are, in short, insignificant. With faith, one can live as he should under any kind of government whatever.

What answers are there, however, for those who are not serious Christians, that is, for the vast majority? I suggest that there are three major ones, and that none of them is tenable.

1. The most idealistic answer is anarchism. If there is no one deserving of power, then no one should be entrusted with power. Government simply should be abolished. But if man is so evil that he cannot under any circumstances use power well, then is he not so evil that power is indispensable for order?

2. The answer that accords most closely with the common sense of Americans is that government should not be given tasks of great importance; individuals should manage their own lives. This position is allied to anarchism, but is less extreme. It is a kind of liberalism. Americans love to hear and repeat liberal slogans damning the government and extolling the self-reliant individual, but their recent experience has pretty much refuted such an outlook. The history of America during the last half-century is largely an account of how a people, in principle deeply suspicious of government, in practice has been compelled greatly to widen its responsibilities.

3. If, due to man's corruptible nature, power cannot be used well, if it is not controlled by God, if it can neither be abolished nor severely limited, then not much remains except to try either to evade the laws and commands of the government or to gain power and use it for selfish advantage. The models of the good life become the criminal and the tyrant.

How near are we today to being left with no answer except the third? No doubt many have a complacent trust in men of power and this keeps their minds clear of the hopelessness represented by the third answer. But these are not generally the most thoughtful and sensitive members of the population. In what direction are students and intellectuals moving? They are told repeatedly that the few are selfish and incompetent, the many vulgar and repressive. Thus, it may be said that, having lost their faith in divine power, they now are losing their faith in human power. If this happens, what remains but despair?

SUGGESTED READINGS

(*Titles are listed chronologically. All are available in paperback or other inexpensive editions.*)

Plato. *Apology* and *Crito*
———. *The Republic*
Aristotle. *Politics,* Books I–IV
Epicurus. *Letters, Principal Doctrines, and Vatican Sayings*
Marcus Aurelius. *Meditations*
Saint Augustine. *The Political Writings of St. Augustine.* Ed. by Henry Paolucci. (Regnery). Chapters 1–3
Saint Thomas Aquinas. *The Political Writings of St. Thomas Aquinas.* Ed. by Dino Bigongiari. (Hafner). Pp. 159–195
Machiavelli Niccolo. *The Prince*
Hobbes, Thomas. *Leviathan,* First and Second Parts
Rousseau, Jean Jacques. *The Social Contract*
Paine, Thomas. *The Rights of Man*
Mill, John Stuart. *Representative Government*
Green, Thomas Hill. *Lectures on the Principles of Political Obligation*
Bosanquet, Bernard. *The Philosophical Theory of the State*
Niebuhr, Reinhold. *Moral Man and Immoral Society*
———. *The Children of Light and the Children of Darkness*
MacIver, R. M. *The Web of Government*
Tillich, Paul. *Love, Power, and Justice*
Jouvenel, Bertrand de. *Sovereignty*
Arendt, Hannah. *The Human Condition*

5

Restraints on Power

Since all power is morally dubious – hard to justify, and likely to corrupt – the confinement of power to its proper bounds is one of the central problems of civilization. Power constantly tends to become arbitrary and limitless. Thus, tyranny is one of the ancient afflictions of man's collective existence. But power has never in history been so boundless and destructive as in some of the totalitarian dictatorships of the twentieth century. These regimes have made it plain that, contrary to Hobbes, not only the lack of a central power but also the lawlessness of a central power renders man's life "solitary, poor, nasty, brutish, and short." To ask about the proper limits on power, and how those limits can be enforced, is to inquire how life can be made decent and civilized.

Limits on power are basically of two kinds: moral and constitutional. Moral limits are those deriving from moral law, or from what men believe to be moral law, and their efficacy depends solely on moral conviction. For a government to refuse to employ murder as an instrument of foreign policy, even though it might have the legal power to do so in certain circumstances, would be an example of a moral limit. Constitutional limits may derive ultimately from a moral law, but what makes them constitutional is their embodiment in a basic law. Such a law, in turn, may either be set down in a certain document, as in America, or it may be merely the content of a general, long-lasting understanding, as in Great Britain. A constitutional government is one that is subject to such a law.

We will discuss each of these kinds of limits beginning with an old and unresolved question concerning morality in politics.

16. Is it justifiable for governments to do evil in order to accomplish good?

One great political thinker, Machiavelli, has argued that it is, and he has become notorious for doing so. We have already spoken of Machiavelli's belief that there can be no order among men and nothing accomplished in human affairs without power. A companion belief, expressed throughout his writing, is that effective use of power is incompatible with strict observance of the moral law. No ideals can be realized without doing evil. It is necessary, if one is to perceive the somewhat tragic coloring of his argument, to understand that Machiavelli never expressed indifference to the moral law and never glorified evil as such. The greatness of Machiavelli's thought depends on the tension inherent in the idea that there is a moral law but that political man occasionally must break it.

By setting forth this point of view Machiavelli gained one of the most unsavory reputations in the history of thought. Among the synonyms for "Machiavellian" that Roget's *Thesaurus* suggests are: "false," "crafty," and "dishonest." Shakespeare referred to "the murderous Machiavel." But while Machiavelli is commonly condemned, no great philosopher has made a serious effort to refute him. The chief works of political thought contain no argument for uncompromising morality that can be set against

Machiavelli's argument that it is justifiable for governments to do evil in order to accomplish good. Many thinkers, such as Plato, Cicero, Thomas Aquinas, and Rousseau, have believed that the health of the political order depends on the moral rectitude of its members. Machiavelli, however, is one of these thinkers; his writings abound in expressions of admiration for the honor and probity of the ancient Romans. He differs from the others only in saying explicitly what they never deny: that while political order depends on respect for moral standards, it depends also on a capacity occasionally to violate those standards. In view of the silence of the great political thinkers concerning an idea so unsettling as this, one wonders whether it is Machiavelli's chief distinction to have divulged a shameful truth (one writer speaks of his "appalling sincerity") that others have been too discreet or too timid to acknowledge.

Opposition to Machiavelli, then, comes less from political philosophy than from common moral convictions. But can people with these convictions hold their ground in the face of political realities such as Machiavelli delineates? For example, let anyone who is repelled by the deceptive and evasive speech common in the political world ask these two questions: (1) Could a government operate successfully if it invariably made public all of its plans and all of its information? (2) Should a government refuse to be deceptive and evasive even if it might thus gain some great good like ending a war or helping an underprivileged group? By reflecting on these questions a person of sensitive conscience may come to agree with Machiavelli that the moral command of full truthfulness cannot be uncompromisingly adhered to in political matters.

Many students and blacks, concerned with righteousness in government, seem to have learned the Machiavellian lesson. For the sake of peace they have introduced chaos into peaceful settings, and to gain dignity for all they have often subjected those in authority to marked indignities.

But lest one acquiesce too readily to Machiavelli's counsel, one should also ask whether *every* moral limit is conditional on political circumstances. If one can lie to reach a political goal, can one kill? Machiavelli defended not only political deceit but also political murder. But if men go this far, what can be left of ideals and conscience? The Communist regimes of Russia and China have been willing to kill in the cause of justice but the consequences so far have been simply more killing and little justice.

The question of the proper moral restraints on power leads to the matter of constitutional restraints. The difference between these two types of restraint, as pointed out above, is that the former is based in moral consciousness, the latter in law. Again, the chief question concerns the wisdom of subjecting governments to invariable limits without regard to variable circumstances.

17. Which should determine the scope of political power, immediate practical considerations or pre-established limitations?

This issue has been forcefully posed by the twentieth-century conflict between democratic and totalitarian nations. During World War II and the early stages of the Cold War it was tempting to see the democracies as the good side and the dictatorships as the bad side. There is a growing realization, however, that good and evil are not so neatly distributed and that there is not only much evil in those countries where the government is restrained by constitutional limitations but that the evil is in some measure protected by the limitations. For example, in the United States, by far the richest country in history, many people are hungry and undernourished. Would this be so if the government's powers of action were not severely restricted by various constitutional bounds?

No political idea in the West has greater authority than that of constitutionalism. For millennia there has been a remarkably wide and persistent consensus that government ought to be carried on within a publicly known and enforceable set of limitations. The great modern spokesman for the concept is John Locke. But Locke is only one of a host of modern thinkers, including Machiavelli, Montesquieu, Burke, Hegel, and John Stuart Mill, who have been firmly committed constitutionalists. Locke's views in this matter were drawn from a solidly established medieval tradition, represented with particular clarity and force by Thomas Aquinas, and this tradition in turn had grown out of a constitutionalist tradition in antiquity, which had been upheld by Plato in his later dialogues, by Aristotle, by Cicero, and by many other ancient thinkers. Few other ideas can claim so impressive a background. Time after time, reaching back to the beginnings of thought, lawless government has been characterized as monstrous and unnatural.

The opposition to this tradition, however, is substantial in the weight of those representing it, if not in numbers. No great thinkers have been exponents of real totalitarianism, that is, of governmental control of every detail of life, but several have been enemies of constitutionalism. Three stand out in the history of thought, and each represents a different motive.

Plato was opposed to constitutionalism because of his faith in the wisdom of a few. Later in his life, when he faced the improbability that these few could ever gain power, he endorsed the idea of constitutional restraints. But earlier, entertaining the notion that philosophers might become kings, he opposed the subjection of government to pre-established limitations. He did this on the logical grounds that perfect wisdom should be free to use power as it sees fit. Plato likened the philosopher-king to a doctor, who is not hamstrung by prior rules but prescribes whatever each unique case requires.

Today we do not have Plato's faith in philosophers. But we do have faith in the Platonic ideal in a more general form – the application of expert intelligence to social problems. Can we in America, with a government confined to limitations established in the eighteenth century, bring to bear on such problems as poverty and urban disorder the full resources of twentieth-century science? This is the kind of question Plato puts before us.

Hobbes was opposed to constitutionalism because of his pessimistic appraisal of man's nature. Numerous passages in Hobbes show that he did not desire anything like modern totalitarianism, but he regarded human beings as far too restless and selfish, too inherently chaotic, to be able to afford governments barred absolutely from certain areas of life. Hobbes' views on religious toleration exemplify this outlook. Hobbes was far from the kind of ideologue or fanatic who wants to impose a single set of beliefs on everyone. He thought it indispensable, nevertheless, that a government have the power to regulate religious creeds and forms of worship. An inviolable rule of toleration would invite men to re-open the "war of all against all."

In quiet American suburbs today Hobbes may seem a mere doctrinaire pessimist. But looking beyond the suburbs, have not the cities, with their poverty and racial tensions, become Hobbesian worlds? And is not the whole globe Hobbesian, split as it is among tense, self-righteous, and heavily armed nations? The impact of such conditions on constitutional government is apparent in the common demand looking to the safety of life and property in the cities, that police have latitude to deal with criminal suspects according to the requirements of immediate circumstances and not be bound by every rule a careful judge might find in the constitution. A very Hobbesian demand!

If Plato opposed constitutionalism out of faith in the few, Rousseau did the same out of faith in the many. A statement like this about Rousseau has to be severely qualified. Rousseau never explicitly attacked constitutional government, and he was passionately committed to the allied idea of rule through law. He thought no command of the sovereign populace valid unless it took the form of law. Nevertheless, the example of Rousseau demonstrates that the idea of government by the people can take on a totalitarian flavor. Just as Plato assumed that no human agency could have the wisdom or right to restrain the most wise and righteous of all men, the philosopher-kings, so Rousseau held that no one could properly impose limitations on the people, except the people themselves. Rousseau's descriptions of the good state show the lives of individuals absorbed into the common life and regulated in detail by the popular will.

Democratic totalitarianism is remote from the spirit and structure of the American Constitution, but it is not hard to see signs of it in the emotions of militant students and blacks. In campus uprisings the normal proceedings of universities have been disrupted, opponents have been shouted down, and "non-negotiable demands" have been put forward. Acts of this kind signify a refusal to abide by the established pattern of restraints for working out disagreements and making decisions. Rebelling students assert that this pattern of restraints is designed to preserve the *status quo* and all of the injustices and inequalities embodied in it. Perhaps this is so, but could there be a perfectly neutral set of restraints? The questions that seem to be posed in the student uprisings are these: Must we choose between equal justice and constitutionalism? And if so, which should we choose?

In sum, although constitutionalism is an ancient tradition, with great moral authority, it is not at all invulnerable to serious doubts. It may be in conflict with three old and eminent ideals: the unrestricted use of scientific knowledge in the solution of social problems, order and peace, and the right of the downtrodden to rise up and claim justice. Is the enforcement of pre-established restraints on power more important than any of these?

At this point it is necessary to ask a question which involves the same basic issues as the question we have just been discussing, but which in form is a completely different question and offers a different perspective on these issues.

18. Should there be only one main center of power in a society?

The reason this question involves the same issues as the one above is that according to a widespread consensus among political thinkers, power can be confined within pre-established limitations only by being divided. Hence, supporters of constitutionalism are invariably supporters also of divided power, while those who favor power which is responsive to immediate practical considerations, unrestrained by pre-established limits, generally favor concentrated power.

This parallelism between the two questions means that the present one requires only brief discussion. It does require discussion, however, both because of its importance in past thought and because of the new vantage point it provides overlooking the region of thought here being explored.

As these observations would lead one to expect, the idea that power should be divided among two or more independent centers rests on a tradition which is no less ancient and authoritative than that supporting the idea of constitutional government. When Plato faced the improbability that philosophers could ever gain power, he concluded that it would be wise to avoid concentrating power in any one group, and that it should be divided between those with characteristics that might indicate wisdom (such as age) and those chosen by lot and thus representing the populace as a whole. With this conception Plato formulated the idea of "the mixed state." During the two-and-a-half millennia it has endured, Plato's idea has taken many forms. But all have expressed the conviction that totally concentrated power menaces decent and civilized existence.

Even Christianity, which one might think would inspire a principle of priestly sovereignty, has its own unique version of the principle of the mixed state. This is the "doctrine of the two swords," which was set forth by the Pope Gelasius near the end of the fifth century and has been adhered to, in some form, by almost every Christian thinker from that time to the present. According to this doctrine, not all power should be in the same hands, not even in the hands of the Pope. Men should not be under the exclusive control of a single sword. True, most Christian thinkers, not only during the Middle Ages but well into modern times, held that there should be only one church, but they did not, for the most part, believe that this one church should hold all power. The ordinary tasks of government, as distinguished from the governance of men's souls to the end of salvation, should be under the authority of a separate sword. Protestant and atheistic critics of the Middle Ages are quick to point out that Christian thinkers were practically never really tolerant and liberal and that the doctrine of the two swords was often construed in a way which set the Church so decisively over the state that the spirit of the doctrine, although not its form, was denied. All of this must be admitted. Nevertheless, the development and the long continuance of the doctrine of the two swords are explicable only on the assumption that even devout Christians, certain as they were that God had spoken clearly and fully, and had authorized a particular human organization to interpret and guard His words, shared the traditional Western mistrust of concentrated power.

America has inherited this mistrust from the Greeks in the form of the separation of powers among the three branches of government and from medieval Christians in the form of the separation of church and state.

But can divided power be effective? Can several competing centers of power accomplish the vast tasks of study, planning, and organization which the swift changes and deep conflicts of this century demand? American history, including as it does long periods of political confusion and governmental deadlock, suggests a negative answer.

Negative answers come forth also from the history of political thought, in spite of the tradition of the mixed state. Every thinker cited above as an opponent of constitutionalism was an opponent also of divided power. For Plato, philosopher-kings would not check one another, for all possessed perfect understanding and could not disagree, and it would be intolerable for them to be checked by men of lesser understanding. For Hobbes, any division of power would be an invitation to the chaos which man's most difficult and important task is to suppress. And for Rousseau, the dispersal of power among separate centers could only mean that the people are not sovereign.

As pointed out in discussing the constitutional limits on power, these thinkers are not out-of-date. They represent attitudes which are powerful in the twentieth century. Plato calls for the comprehensive and organized use of scientific knowledge in solving social problems, Hobbes for the utmost efficiency in keeping order, and Rousseau for the unchecked ascendancy of the people. All of these demands are insistently voiced in our time, and all, at least implicitly, are demands for concentrated power. Are there good grounds for resisting them, or must we become witnesses to the collapse of the ancient tradition of the mixed state?

To carry forward our thinking about constitutionalism one thing needs particular attention, freedom. For many people on both sides the crux of the matter is freedom. The authority of the constitutionalist and mixed state tradition derives primarily, in modern times, from the assumption that constitutionalism assures, or at least is among the prerequisites of, freedom. On the other side, much of the opposition to this tradition comes from the conviction that constitutionalism does not bring freedom, or brings only a paltry freedom. Many student rebels, for example, regard human life under the American constitutional system as so trivialized and debased that it is not in any significant way free. Hence, what we must consider are the relations between constitutionalism and freedom.

19. Are men who live under a constitutional government necessarily free?

Three general answers to this question can be readily distinguished:

First, freedom is simply a state of not being subject to arbitrary and excessive requirements on the part of the government. Thus, the answer to the question is yes. Those who live under a constitutional government – a government barred from imposing arbitrary and excessive requirements – are necessarily free. The main prerequisite of freedom is an effective constitution.

Second, freedom is a state of not being subject to arbitrary and excessive requirements from any source whatever, from a government, an employer, a relative, or anyone else. One might live under a constitutional government and still be subject to the despotic acts of an employer who can take away one's livelihood. Freedom depends not on constitutional government alone but on a social order in which every major power, whether governmental or otherwise, is held within pre-established limitations. Fair employment practices legislation exemplifies the effort to impose such limitations on businessmen.

Third, freedom is not simply the absence of arbitrary interference; it is the capacity for action. One might live not only under a constitutional government but in a society in which every power is under pre-established restraints and still be unfree. This would be the case if one were unemployed or illiterate. It would be the case also if one lived in a society that provided few opportunities for creative action such as in the arts or in business. Freedom, then, depends on a whole set of political, personal, and social conditions.

These three conceptions of freedom, by implication, are conceptions also of the role of government power. According to the first, the main demand to be placed on government is that, aside from performing certain minimal tasks, it leave people alone. According to the second conception, however, in which freedom is construed as the absence of interference from any source whatever, government might (to use the phrase of an English political philosopher, Bernard Bosanquet) "hinder hindrances" to freedom. Does it not do this if it passes effective fair employment practices legislation? Finally, the third conception, that of freedom as the capacity for action, suggests even wider uses of power for creating the conditions of freedom. A government might enlarge the areas of freedom by establishing adult education programs or mental health centers.

Such apparently dry distinctions define the front lines of many of the great political battles of the twentieth century. In the terms commonly used in present-day American political controversy, "conservatives" are those who adhere to the Lockean conception of freedom and maintain that constitutionalism is the principal condition of freedom. "Liberals" argue that freedom depends on a government that is not only subject to constitutional restraints but that also protects freedom against interference on the part of any nongovernmental power, such as industry or finance. The third conception of freedom and of the role of government cannot be quite so definitely labeled, but roughly speaking it is the conception held by "radicals." Freedom is held to depend on a completely new environment. To create that environment, a completely different kind of government than that envisioned by conservatives and liberals is needed.

These issues have arisen primarily from one of the critical events in all of history, the industrial revolution. In the pre-industrial era it was relatively easy to assume that freedom was simply life under a constitutional government because, after the disintegration of the Catholic Church in the age of the Reformation, government was the largest established power. If it did not threaten freedom, presumably freedom was not threatened. With the industrial revolution, however, great industrial and financial organizations, not controlled by government but often themselves controlling governments, came into existence. It was obvious that such organizations might deprive individuals of their freedom and they did. A laborer in London, for example, might have had to work sixteen hours every day, his working conditions were likely to leave him in a few years ruined in health, his living quarters were probably filthy and crowded, and his wife and children might have been not only hungry and sick but themselves also under the necessity of working for many hours every day. In Locke's terms, such a man was free, but it was plain to "liberals" (the term having been defined broadly enough to include many of those who, in England, called themselves "socialists"), that he was not free, in fact, but might become so if the government, beyond observing certain restraints in its own action, were to see that his employer did the same.

Until fairly recently, both in England and America, the "liberals" seemed destined to vanquish the "conservatives" completely. It appeared that a well-informed and humane person had to be "liberal." Today, however, the situation is not so clear. The primary reason for this is that the results of governmental efforts to "hinder hindrances" to freedom have been disappointing. Such efforts have not failed altogether, but they have failed for certain groups, such as the black people in America, and they have not created for anyone wholly admirable and heartening societies. The poverty and squalor of the average black person's life in America today, and the dullness and demoralization of Socialist Britain, exemplify the conditions that have brought disenchantment with liberalism.

Disenchantment, of course, is not refutation. One argument in behalf of liberalism is that it has failed only where it has not been applied. It has not remedied racial injustice in America, for example, simply because conservatives so far have successfully resisted the adequate use of governmental power in the protection of civil liberties. Arguments of this kind are plausible, but they no longer seem conclusive. Liberals are now on the defensive.

On one side, the notion that freedom depends on the initiative of individuals rather than of governments, and that the main condition of freedom is simply constitutionalism, has gained a new plausibility, making room for the kind of conservatism which merely opposes every call for governmental action and takes no responsibility for the problems with which liberals are concerned. But it also makes room for a more progressive view that sees private individuals as joining together and, while perhaps accepting governmental assistance but not relying on it, creating the conditions of their own freedom. This view seems to be inherent in some segments at least of both Hippie culture and the black power movement. When blacks, for example, organize a boycott against stores involved in overpricing they are moving on their own to claim freedom, but not according to typical liberal tactics.

On the other side, liberals are attacked by a far more vociferous and self-confident radicalism than they have ever faced before. Distinctions here cannot be drawn with a sharpness that places every person definitely in one category and in no other. It might be difficult, for example, to know whether some Hippies should be classified under the antigovernmental progressivism suggested in the paragraph above or under the radicalism we are speaking of here. Nevertheless, setting aside problems of individual classification and looking at society as a whole, the radical attitude is dramatically evident, especially among campus militants. It betrays no hostility to government as such, but it reveals a commitment to social transformation of such depth and swiftness as no government of the American type, and perhaps no constitutional government whatever, could bring about. It reveals also a desire for government that is far more decentralized and democratic than the typical constitutional regime. One breathes here the atmosphere of totalitarian democracy that was noted in discussing Rousseau.

Let us summarily restate the issues: Does constitutionalism assure freedom? Is it merely a prerequisite, with freedom dependent in addition on governmental action or group initiative? Or is constitutionalism an obstacle to freedom? Many Americans will be forced to answer these questions, in one way or another, almost every day in coming years.

The idea of government under pre-established limits, and that of government without such limits, are alike unsatisfactory. The former implies that good rulers will be hindered, the latter that bad rulers will not; the former means compromise and delay in carrying out the best of plans, the latter expeditious accomplishment of the worst. It is not surprising that from the beginnings of political thought men have sought to avoid both horns of the dilemma and to discover how government might be restrained from doing evil but not from doing good. One might think of several possible solutions, such as arranging matters so that the interests of rulers and ruled are identical. But one possible solution stands out from the others for its simplicity and appeal. Government might be restrained from doing what it ought not to do, but not from what it ought to do, by being placed in the hands of men pre-eminent in understanding. In short, constitutions might be replaced by science, or by revelation. Is there any validity in such a notion?

20. Can governments ever be made the servants of perfect knowledge?

Flawless, all-inclusive knowledge has been the object of persisting hope. Plato expressed this hope in his ideal of the philosopher, of the man who had, by reasoning, gained knowledge of "the Good." Many medieval and Reformation Christians believed that such knowledge had been bestowed on man, who could never have reasoned his way to it, through Christ. In modern times, faith in Christ has declined but faith in reason, comparable in its intensity to Plato's, has been reawakened by the progress of science.

Can governments ever be made the servants of such knowledge? The idea that they can has naturally accompanied the hope that perfect knowledge might be attained. Plato thought philosophers should become kings. Medieval Christians were continually tempted, in spite of the doctrine of the two swords, to grant the Pope a power as limitless and unified as they believed Christian revelation to be. The modern political imagination has long been fascinated by the idea of technocracy, government carried on by masters of technology and science.

The idea of joining power and perfect knowledge perhaps has serious flaws, but at the very least it is noble and attractive. It represents that ineradicable feeling we discussed in connection with constitutionalism that it is one of the greatest of all evils to be helplessly subject to the whims and ignorance of another human being. The idea of constitutionalism is that rulers should be compelled to stay within certain legal boundaries. The idea of subordinating government to perfect knowledge is much more radical. It proposes that the very willfulness and ignorance which necessitate legal boundaries be eliminated. It envisions the destruction of arbitrary government at its roots in human nature. What constitutionalism would merely check – capriciousness and stupidity – perfect knowledge would totally exterminate.

The notion that this is possible, however, rests on two assumptions: first, that perfect knowledge is available, at least to some men; and second, that this knowledge has the power of determining the behavior of its possessors, thus transmitting to them, as it were, its own perfection. Both of these assumptions have been frequently challenged.

As for the first, one of the most noticeable qualities of thought during the last century or two has been what might be called "epistemological discouragement," that is, discouragement over the possibilities of gaining sure and comprehensive knowledge (*epistēmē*, in the Greek). The medieval and Reformation faith that God has given man such knowledge of his origin, nature, and end is weak if not dead. Optimistic churchmen may cite figures showing increasing church attendance, but even the churchmen themselves are more likely to study man by reading social science than by pondering the New Testament.

It is often said that faith has been defeated by science. The strange fact is, however, that modern man has not only lost faith in Christian revelation but in science as well. Everyone of course would agree that scientists have made striking discoveries. The question is whether these reveal reality itself or only certain relations among our perceptions of reality. As early as the eighteenth century David Hume (1711–1776) argued that neither observation nor reasoning can possibly demonstrate the reality of those universal and invariable laws which supposedly make up the content of science. Immanuel Kant (1724–1804) attempted to answer Hume and to show that true and certain knowledge is possible. According to Kant, however, the scientific laws which make up this knowledge are derived not from reality itself but from the structure of the human mind. Kant argued that being itself is completely unknowable. Thus, Kant's defense of science was highly equivocal. He asserted that men can frame absolutely valid scientific laws, but these manifest the conditions of human understanding and not the nature and motions of reality itself.

It is generally agreed that Kant is one of the greatest thinkers of all time. Also, he has been one of the most influential, and is the source of much of our "epistemological discouragement." Probably the most dramatic contemporary sign of Kant's influence, and of the weakness of modern man's faith in science, is existentialism. Many different outlooks have been called "existentialist." One central idea is common to all of them, however, and that is simply that man is not an object of knowledge. He is essentially a subject, one who knows. When he is treated as an object, something that is known, he is distorted and, thus, is not really known. If this is so, then nothing remotely like the perfect, changeless knowledge envisioned by Plato, and by many admirers of modern science, is available.

A number of serious and able people do not agree with Hume, Kant, and other critics of human reason. No one, however, would deny that these critics have done much to set the mood of the twentieth century, a mood in which both the medieval ideal of Christian knowledge, and the Greek and modern ideal of rational knowledge, seems dubious. A sensitive person cannot help wondering at times whether we can know anything at all, except, perhaps, that we inhabit an impenetrable darkness.

But in asking whether governments can ever become the servants of perfect knowledge we must not only ask whether such knowledge can ever be gained, we must ask also whether, if it could be gained, men would be disposed to respect it. It is at least conceivable that mankind might know all things yet still be stupidly and brutally governed. It is not obvious that perfect knowledge means perfect virtue.

Some men, however, have held that an equation of this kind can be made. Socrates apparently believed that full knowledge – that is, knowledge of man's nature and needs, and knowledge of what is really good – leads inevitably to moral excellence. If one knows, fully and certainly, what is good he is bound to choose it. Therefore, an evil man must be an ignorant man. Thus, knowledge cannot possibly be misused. This identification of knowledge and virtue strongly influenced Plato and modern men as well. It implies that it is completely safe to put limitless power in the hands of those with perfect knowledge, and was a major premise underlying Plato's concept of the philosopher-king. It implies also that a society with much knowledge is bound to live well, and through this implication it supports the modern assumption that the progress of science must entail the general improvement of life.

In recent decades, however, this assumption has come to appear increasingly dubious. We seem to have gained vast quantities of knowledge, through both the physical sciences and the social sciences, but we appear as likely to use this knowledge for evil ends, like nuclear warfare and "brainwashing," as for good ends like the elimination of poverty. It is easy to feel now that we are menaced, rather than saved, by our knowledge. If this is so, is it because our knowledge is still imperfect and incomplete, so that it is necessary for the social sciences to "catch up" with the physical sciences? Or is it because Socrates was wrong and it is possible for individuals and peoples to be masters of knowledge but still selfish and cruel?

While Socrates apparently argued that every effort of life should be centered on knowing good and evil, the Book of Genesis suggests mythically that this is the very heart of sin. Adam was cast out of Paradise after he and Eve, tempted by the serpent, had tasted fruit from "the tree of the knowledge of good and evil." It seems fair to symbolize the dilemma of our civilization in terms of these two great sources of understanding. One exalts the human mind and leads logically to the ideal of government directed and restrained by a knowledge comprehending all needs and all means to their satisfaction. The other humbles us and tells us that as long as we seek to be "as gods, knowing good and evil," we will suffer the anguish of labor, estrangement, and mortality. What failure has brought us to the despair and disorder of the twentieth century – following Socrates inadequately or the serpent too readily?

SUGGESTED READINGS

(*Titles are listed chronologically. All are available in paperback or other inexpensive editions.*)

Plato. *The Republic*
Cicero, Marcus Tullius. *On the Commonwealth*
Saint Thomas Aquinas. *The Political Writings of St. Thomas Aquinas*. Ed. by Dino Bigongiari. (Hafner). Pp. 175–195
Machiavelli, Niccolo. *The Discourses*
Hobbes, Thomas. *Leviathan*, Second Part
Locke, John. *The Second Treatise of Government*
Rousseau, Jean Jacques. *The Social Contract*
Hamilton, Jay, and Madison. *The Federalist*
Bosanquet, Bernard. *The Philosophical Theory of the State*
Ruggiero, Guido do. *The History of European Liberalism*
Wheare, K. C. *Modern Constitutions*
Lippmann, Walter. *The Public Philosophy*

6

The Ends of Power

Power must be used as well as restrained. Thus, political thinking involves reflection on the ends of power. Most of the great political thinkers (Machiavelli is one of the exceptions) have devoted much attention to this subject, which is difficult to consider because it incorporates two large and refractory problems. First, what are the ends of human life in general? Clearly one cannot decide what tasks government should perform unless he has developed some notion of the purpose of life in general. But this has been an enigma for every generation. Some of the thinkers of our own day – Jean-Paul Sartre and his followers – have reached the seemingly despairing conclusion that human life has no purpose whatever. One must also deal with a second intractable question: What sort of tasks can power accomplish? Having identified the ends of life, it is necessary to try to estimate what power can do to help reach them. Thus, thought concerning the ends of power can go astray in two ways – by misconstruing the ends of life and by misunderstanding the capacities of power.

The importance of thinking about the ends of power, however, matches the difficulty of doing so, particularly today, when there is deep confusion concerning the purposes of men and governments. This confusion is probably caused by several conditions, such as our lack of faith either in revelation or in reason, the subjection of the social order to repeated, unforeseeable rearrangements brought about by technology, and the permeation of thought and feeling with the fads cultivated by commercialized television. The political consequences of the confusion may well be severe. At the very least it will lead to the devotion of resources and attention to secondary problems, such as exploration of space rather than elimination of poverty, and at worst, to an effort to escape the burden of discord and uncertainty by placing absolute power in the hands of a leader or party claiming superhuman insight. In one way or another, if we sink unprotestingly into a state of doubt and indifference regarding the ends of power, those ends are likely to be set by irresponsible and insensitive men who feel themselves unchecked by the moral and political consciousness of other men.

For these reasons it is not a leisured diversion but an urgent and practical duty to reflect on the ends of power. The first idea that is likely to occur to anyone who attempts to do so is that the good at which power aims should be a common good, one shared by all. But it is doubtful whether there ever is a single good shared by all of the millions making up a society. Therefore, it is appropriate to ask at the outset whether every government does not necessarily pursue the good of only a portion of the society, that portion controlling the government.

21. Does every government serve merely "the interest of the stronger"?

The phrase, "the interest of the stronger," and the argument that it describes the end of every government, is attributed to Thrasymachus in Plato's *Republic*. Thrasymachus assumed that men are estranged in essence. Hence, there is no such thing as "the common good" or "the general welfare." The ends of each man are not only solely his own, and not the ends of anyone else; they are likely to be in conflict with the ends of others. Every man with power consequently seeks his own good alone and sacrifices the welfare of others to attain it. It follows that even the most ancient and venerated order of society and state, claiming as societies usually have the sanction both of God and the people, is only a great fraud. It purports to be an embodiment of the interest of all; it is in fact only a device by which men with power get what they want.

Probably none of the great thinkers has wholly agreed with Thrasymachus, but some of them have been so deeply suspicious of established governments that they have assumed that most of them do, in fact, serve merely "the interest of the stronger," even though there might be some exceptional condition – such as philosophers becoming kings – which would enable them to do otherwise. Marx exemplified this attitude. He, of course, believed that the working class was destined to rise up and seize power from the owning class. When this happened government would be carried on so completely and obviously in the interest of all that it would no longer even be a coercive institution, and the state would "wither away." Prior to this event, however, every government is inescapably a tyranny of the propertied groups. All laws, all actions of the government, even the artistic, religious, and philosophical works that define the reigning culture, are on the whole shaped, consciously or unconsciously, to further the power and aims of the dominant class. Such devices as written constitutions, representative assemblies, and popular elections, which supposedly compel governments to respect the freedom and interests of their subjects, are fraudulent. They are only ways of veiling the dictatorship of the owners. Thus, Marx qualified Thrasymachus only by adding, "until the Communist revolution"; otherwise he wholly agreed that the "justice" maintained by governments is nothing but the "interest of the stronger."

It would hardly be too much to say that refuting Thrasymachus has been the principal aim of political thought. Plato devoted the whole of *The Republic* to this task. (Presumably men who agreed wholly with Thrasymachus have concentrated on some more promising way of exploiting their fellow men than writing political philosophy.) Of course, not all thinkers have had Thrasymachus consciously in mind, but almost all of them have tried to show that government can further some state of things that is not merely in the interest of the stronger but of all. Even so cynical a thinker as Hobbes argued emphatically that peace is good for everyone, and men like Rousseau and Marx, who thought that governments rarely if ever pursued the common good, nevertheless concentrated on showing how their selfishness might be transcended. When recent liberalism, in response to Marxist criticism, tried to show that liberal and democratic regimes could act in the interest of workers as well as of owners they were simply renewing the ancient effort to refute Thrasymachus.

But can it be done? This probably depends on whether it can be shown, in answer to question 1, that men are essentially united. In even a just society some members must get less – of leisure, job satisfaction, wealth, and so forth – than they would like to have. This is strikingly true of soldiers who lose their lives in battle, of workers who perform indispensable but stultifying jobs, and of criminals who are caught. The problem is to show that such people are not, in every conceivable case, merely the weak being sacrificed in the interest of the strong. This is possible only if all are essentially so at one that those who sacrifice conscious desires for the common good actually sacrifice those desires for their own highest good and are not merely means to the welfare of others.

Most students react with doubt, if not hostility, when confronted with this argument. It is not as far from common sense, however, as it may seem to be. We do not generally think of a soldier who has lost his life in war (unless it be an unjust war, such as, perhaps, that in Viet Nam) as merely a weak man victimized by the strong. Nor do we think in this way of a criminal spending time in prison. The fate of each is felt to be in some way justified. It is felt to serve some end, such as the survival of the nation or the maintenance of justice, which is taken as more important to each person even than his life. Not that people always feel this way, but they ordinarily do under governments based on consent. They have in America, at least up to the present time.

But instead of getting involved in such far-fetched speculations, can we not merely say that each one of us has his own interests but that these do here and there coincide? It is very doubtful that we can. The *conscious* interests of millions of people are never the same. Not even such elemental goods as order and peace are desired by absolutely everyone. Every revolution and war provide examples of people who profit from chaos. Every social order, therefore, depends on some coercion, usually in the form of subtle pressure, occasionally of open force. This coercion must be simply an assertion of "the interest of the stronger" unless it is exercised in behalf of some ultimate common good, which, being common, is the good of those coerced, but, since they must be coerced, is not perceived by them. In short, since people cannot be at one in their *conscious* interests, they must be at one in their *ultimate* interests. Either that, or every government serves merely "the interest of the stronger."

The issue of moral absolutism *versus* moral relativism, described briefly in the second chapter,[1] is closely linked with this question. If there are absolute moral laws, or absolute values, then these must in some way define a common good. For example, a moral absolutist might regard justice as a good to which every purely individual interest is properly subordinate, the view of both Plato and Rousseau. However, if all moral rules and all values are relative to circumstances or persons then it is questionable whether the idea of a truly common good makes sense. It may be that a moral relativist is logically bound to take the side of Thrasymachus. Certainly Plato's attack on Thrasymachus was an attack on moral relativism in general. However, the paths of thought are intricate enough to make the assertion of any absolute rule in this matter inadvisable. Many relativists, cer-

[1] See above, pp. 22–23.

tainly, have been no less antagonistic to Thrasymachus' viewpoint than was Plato.

In speculating on this question we are traversing what is probably the most rugged and uninviting terrain in the whole realm of political theory. But there is no way of passing around it. A political system is essentially a set of arrangements by which some people dominate others. How can this be made morally tolerable? All civilized life is carried on under a great moral shadow. More explicitly, all civilized life must be assumed to rest on exploitation of the weak, unless we can show that Thrasymachus was wrong and that all "justice" is not merely the way dominant groups get what they want.

At this point let it be assumed that the present question has been answered negatively, thus establishing by implication the principle that governments can and should serve the common good. What is this good? Is it a spiritual good, such as faith or moral excellence? It has often been asserted in the past that it is. Plato's ideal of philosophical rule, for example, was an ideal of power used for spiritual ends. But during the past few centuries people have become increasingly reluctant to allow the government any spiritual functions. Correspondingly, they have stressed the urgency of material aims and recently have asserted a heavy governmental responsibility in this regard. Hence, it may be easier for us to begin reflecting at the material, rather than the spiritual, end of the spectrum of political values. Accordingly, let us consider whether, as many conscientious people in recent times have believed, governments should take on the task of directing the economic order.

22. Should governments appropriate the major facilities for production and distribution?

This question concerns man's responsibility for the earth, or for the whole material setting of human life and all the materials that can be used for the improvement of life.

An old idea, accepted by both Locke and Marx, the fathers respectively of "free enterprise" and "socialism," and derived perhaps from the Old Testament, is that the earth is the common possession of mankind. By some primal right, established by God or "nature," it belongs to all. But how can mankind actually take the earth into its possession and use it – by allowing individuals freely to appropriate parts of it or by placing it in the custody of governments?

The answer accepted in one way or another by all defenders of capitalism was given by Locke when he asserted that "the Condition of Humane life, which requires Labour and Materials to work on, necessarily introduces *private Possessions*."[2] While the earth *belongs* to mankind, it can be *used* only by individuals. Hence, it must be appropriated by individuals. Government has the duty of protecting individuals in their use of the earth – of protecting, that is, the rights of property. But it has no direct responsibility for the earth. It must only protect the private persons who do have such a responsibility.

But is it true that efficient use of the earth requires individual appropriation? Does not the history of industrialism indicate, on the contrary, that our exploitation of the earth depends on immense economic organizations and that the individual alone can do almost nothing? Locke asserts that a man has the right to keep "the Acorns he picks up under an Oak, or the Apples he gathered from the Trees in the Wood."[3] But have such examples any relevance to the economic order of the twentieth century? Today in America there is scarcely a single item of daily use that is the product of individual labor. Our cars, clothing, food, household utensils, and so forth all come out of vast systems coordinating individual effort and skill.

Furthermore, does not the history of capitalism indicate that free appropriation by some entails complete deprivation for many others? It has, of course, been urged that those who are

[2] Locke, *op. cit.*, p. 310. The italics are Locke's.
[3] *Ibid.*, p. 306.

able to appropriate a great deal demonstrate by this very ability their right to all that they appropriate, while those who have nothing thus prove that they deserve nothing. But it is certainly a suspicious logic that begins with the principle of man's common ownership of the earth and concludes with the principle that a minority can rightfully appropriate all of the earth for themselves. It is not surprising that this logic has not been universally accepted.

Socialism, in the broadest sense, represents the simple idea that mankind must assert its primal right to the earth by actually taking the earth into its possession and using it cooperatively. Socialists have not agreed whether this should be done through governmental action or in some other way. There are several kinds of socialism, but what unites them all is an unwillingness to tolerate private appropriation of the earth.

It seems fair to say that in practice common appropriation has nearly always meant governmental appropriation. Moreover, it is hard to see how it can mean anything else. An economic enterprise might, of course, be taken over by a cooperative group smaller than the whole society. A factory, for example, might be run by the workers. But this is not really common ownership. A private group, even though composed of workers, may be exclusive and selfish. An anarchist strain in socialism is expressed in the anticipation that societies will appropriate and use the earth through spontaneous cooperation. Communists, for example, looked forward to "the withering away of the state." As everyone knows, the very opposite has occurred in all Communist nations. If all of us together are to appropriate the earth, it seems that this must be done through the one agency that represents all of us together, that is, the government.

The trouble is, of course, that for the government to own something is not the least bit the same as for everyone together to own it. Not that governmental ownership, which must mean governmental responsibility for the production, use, and distribution of material wealth, is necessarily unwise. It may possibly lead to greater efficiency, since an industrial economy is an elaborately integrated system and must have some measure of centralized direction. It may also lead to greater justice, for the government can insist that the profit-seeking activities of individuals be subordinated to some widely accepted conception of the common good. Even if these advantages are realized, however, the fact remains that governmental direction of the economy, with the powerful officialdom and pervasive bureaucratic procedures that inevitably go with it, is far from the ideal of common appropriation which is the moral foundation of socialism. It must be obvious to any private citizen in Russia that governmental ownership of industries is not even an approximation to ownership by himself and his fellow citizens. And this is not just because the government of Russia is a dictatorship. It does not appear that the people in democratic England, either, have much feeling that the coal mines and railroads are common possessions.

There is one way, indeed, in which governmental control of the economy may be even further from common ownership than a regime of private ownership. Governmental control unites the political and economic centers of power. Thus, these do not check one another, as they occasionally do within a capitalist system, and the power over the people may be more concentrated and uncontrollable than it would be under a system of private ownership.

In this kind of impasse the common sense of the typical American immediately suggests that the truth is somewhere between the two extremes. And indeed such a suggestion is not without weight. In the history of political thought it is probably Thomas Aquinas (1225?–1274?) who has most clearly delineated a theory of property that sanctions neither unrestrained individual appropriation nor total governmental control. Aquinas argued that property should be held by individuals but that it should be regulated by law and custom to assure its being used in the common interest. He maintained, as an American businessman might, that a man will much more carefully look after what is his own than what is held in common, and the economy will be more efficiently managed under a system of private property than under any other system. At the same time, Aquinas condemned the use of property primarily for personal profit. It should be used for the common good, and society has a right to see that it is. On this side of his thought Aquinas seems less like an American businessman than like the socialist and leftist whom the businessman would excoriate as dangerous radicals.

Is the issue thus resolved? No one should quickly conclude that it is. In actual political practice, it may often be sagacious to profess a middle position, but in political thinking to do so is often just a way of avoiding issues. Thus, one must ask whether the Thomist position resolves the dilemma created by the individualistic and socialistic theories of appropriation or whether it merely obscures it. There is room for doubt. Does the right of individual property mean that an individual can, if he insists, appropriate and use some significant part of the earth according to his own desires and contrary to the will of society? If it does mean this, then what is ostensibly an intermediate position seems in essence to be an individualism like that made explicit by Locke. If it does not mean this, however, and the individual's use of his property can be supervised and controlled by society, then it is questionable how much the right of individual ownership actually means. In substance, the theory would seem to be one of common ownership. If, finally, it is sometimes the individual and sometimes society that is responsible for the earth, then it must be explained exactly where the line between the two is to be drawn and how disputes between them are to be refereed.

The question as to whether individuals should be free to appropriate the earth has always been important, but it has never been as important as it is today, because technology has placed the earth much more fully at man's disposal than it has ever been before. The right of individual appropriation is a much more sweeping power than it was in the days of Locke. Private persons have used the earth in ways that have decisively affected whole nations. The lives of the American people, for example, have probably been shaped as significantly in the twentieth century by General Motors as by the Supreme Court. Is it right, then, that General Motors should be private property? On the other hand, the immensity of the powers entailed in the ownership of certain kinds of property may be the very fact that makes one unwilling to resort to governmental appropriation. Is there any way, having developed the power to work spectacular and devastating effects on the earth, of fulfilling the spirit of the biblical assertion that "the heaven, even the heavens, are the Lord's: but the earth hath he given to the children of men"? [4]

But "man does not live by bread only," and while twentieth-century America has been preoccupied with material goals, other societies and other ages have been concerned mainly with goals of the spirit, such as faith and morality. The time may have come when Americans are ready to reconsider their relationship to such goals. Many have gained material plenty and have found it not only insufficient but even stultifying and demoralizing.

Of course, Americans generally have held that individuals can pursue spiritual aims if they wish to but that government must have absolutely nothing to do with such efforts. It must be remembered, however, that there are many ways in which government influences the minds of citizens. The examples set by public officials, the words of charismatic leaders, the legal sanctioning of certain kinds of human relations (such as integration of the races), and the philosophical and moral attitudes inculcated by public education are among the ways governments commonly exert spiritual influence. They suffice to show that to consider the spiritual responsibilities of government is not necessarily to toy with the idea of totalitarian dictatorship. It is far from the only alternative to the total severence of the spiritual and political that Americans now profess.

[4] Psalm 115:16.

As examples of spiritual goals we have mentioned faith and morality, the great ideals respectively of the Middle Ages and the ancient world. Let us consider these in turn, substituting for the word "faith" a word that seems less restrictive and less anachronistic.

23. Should governments assume responsibility for shaping the beliefs of individuals?

The average American is so sure of the answer to this question that he is likely to be surprised that the question is even asked. The same intelligent and humane man who is convinced that the government has responsibility for the material welfare of individuals is equally convinced that it has no responsibility whatever for their spiritual welfare. Who is to say what beliefs are true? And if someone must say, why should it not be each individual, deciding for himself? The individualism that was once axiomatic in economic matters has now become axiomatic in spiritual matters.

This is perhaps a very good thing. It seems worth noting, however, that on the whole the great thinkers of the past have not been of the same mind, and they have not shared our spiritual individualism or our political secularism. The idea that government should be wholly detached in matters of belief, and the individual left completely on his own, developed fairly recently, only two or three hundred years ago. Locke defended such a doctrine near the end of the seventeenth century. He was not the first to do so, but he spoke for an idea that was still controversial and generally unacceptable.

Moreover, the reasons earlier thinkers had for asserting some governmental responsibility for beliefs were not absurd. They may have been inadequate, but they were not incomprehensible or manifestly unreasonable. To begin with, they thought that we can know with assurance what the truth is. The question "Who is to say?" asked by many students today would have been attributed, by most of the great Greek and medieval thinkers, as well as by a number of early modern thinkers, to laziness, confusion, or something else blinding them to the importance and availability of objective truth about man and the universe. But why not leave the determination of this truth to each individual? Most of these thinkers would have made the sensible, although possibly erroneous, response that discovery of the truth is difficult even for the greatest minds and that it is altogether beyond the capacity of average minds. Consequently, if government and society give no help to the individual in deciding what he will believe, the result for most people will be uncertainty and despair. The result for society, since social order depends on some beliefs being held firmly and in common, will be weakness and disorder.

Most thinkers of the past would not have inferred from these arguments that the government should have an exclusive and unchecked right to proclaim the truth. They would not have inferred that the government should try to uphold the truth with violence and terror. Aristotle, for example, assumed that scientists and philosophers independent of the government had primary responsibility for finding the truth and making it known, and the typical medieval thinker believed that supervision of belief was a duty pertaining first of all to the spiritual sword rather than to the temporal. And even Plato and Augustine, who were more radical and passionate than men like Aristotle, were far from desiring to see the truth promoted by force. Education was the way taught by Plato, and Augustine only after long hesitation and with utmost reluctance sanctioned the use of violence against heretics.

But none of these thinkers, and few others until recent times, came near the modern idea that government is spiritually neutral. To know the truth was for them one of man's principal aims, and government was far too great an influence in human life to be barred from participating in the common pursuit of this aim.

It is noteworthy that Locke based his individualism, in economic and spiritual matters alike, on the same broad principles, and that the typical American liberal has rejected these principles in regard to property but clings to them in regard to belief. Thus, in the first place, Locke assumed a certain essential estrangement among men. This means, economically, that the use one man makes of his own property is not the business of anyone else. It means, spiritually, that the beliefs of one man are of no proper concern to another man. Further, Locke assumed that there is a natural harmony among individuals. Thus, he thought, if each one gains and uses property according to the dictates of his own interests, order and prosperity will naturally ensue. Likewise, in the spiritual realm, if each man believes what he chooses, the truth will emerge spontaneously. Finally, Locke had the kind of conception of freedom which I characterized above as "negative." It comports with his theory of property to say that one is economically free if he is not being interfered with in the accumulation and use of property even though, as a matter of fact, he may have so little property that he is starving. Correspondingly, Locke apparently considered a man to be spiritually free if his beliefs, even though false, were of his own choosing.

When the typical liberal is considering economic questions he is likely to assume (1) that men are not essentially estranged but that each has some responsibility for the welfare of all others; (2) that there is no natural harmony, but that unrestrained accumulation of profits by individuals leads to drastic inequalities and to cycles of inflation and depression, and that a just and stable economic order consequently depends on governmental action; and (3) that freedom to starve is not real freedom. And yet in matters of personal belief the same liberal is likely to remain an unreconstructed Lockean liberal. Is there an underlying logic holding together his seemingly divided consciousness?

In order to test his views on this question, it might help the student to imagine that a belief he detests – for example, that white men constitute a superior race, or that America should be organized and governed by the military – has won the allegiance of a large and powerful group in the country. Would he object if the government took steps to assure that this belief was not taught in the public schools or proclaimed without opposition in the nation's press?

Let us turn to a final dimension of men's spiritual life, morality. Men of antiquity were less concerned than we are today with material welfare and less preoccupied than most people in the Middle Ages with faith. But they were greatly concerned with morality, not as a puritanical discipline denying worldly pleasure for the sake of life after death but as a wisdom for living fully within this world. Correspondingly, government stood, as they viewed it, in a position of moral authority. Does this view too greatly elevate political leadership?

24. Should governments assume responsibility for shaping the moral character of individuals?

For most people today the answer to this question is as emphatic a negative as the answer to the preceding question. To begin with, moral theories are very dubious. Anyone who presumes to say what is good and evil is putting forth a mere personal opinion, which he cannot prove and, thus, should not be able to force upon others. The notion that governments should define the good life and impose it on people is particularly outrageous, for governments are not wiser than private people. On the contrary, they are often uniquely crude and uncomprehending. Each individual should be allowed to shape his own life. If morality is the capacity for living well, then one man has as good a claim to being moral as another. Each one has his own ideas as to what it means to live well. No one has a right to set himself over others and tell them how to live. Besides, even if it were right for the government to try to make men moral, how could it? A moral action is one that is freely done, whereas all the government can do is coerce. An act done under governmental pressure could not possibly be moral.

These are very familiar attitudes in twentieth-century America.

They are not baseless or arbitrary. One can discern beneath them some of the basic principles of modern liberalism, such as moral relativism, individualism, egalitarianism, and the idea that government belongs on the periphery of life and not at its center.

However, the other side – the notion that government does have some responsibility for shaping the moral character of individuals – is represented by thinkers of the stature of Aristotle and Thomas Aquinas and thus is not as unsound as many Americans would suppose. In Aristotle, the argument amounts to something like the following chain of principles: living well is not just doing as one pleases but depends on understanding and adhering to a pattern of life which, in a general way, is valid for all men; discovery of this pattern depends on unusual insight and cannot be accomplished by ordinary men; most people, therefore, depend on society to give moral structure to their lives; government, as the principal agent of society, must see that society's moral responsibilities are carried out. This is not to say that a government should decide all by itself what is moral and then force it on people. Government should be the agent of a moral consciousness that is the mind and tradition of a whole culture and not merely the creation of a government; and its moral influence should be wielded less through coercion than through example, through education, and through the respect, rather than fear, inspired by the laws.

These two views of the moral responsibility of government (we may call them the "liberal" and "moralistic" views) involve two very different conceptions of law. In the liberal view the principal function of law is protection. The law should provide security for person and property and assure the individual a sphere in which he can live as he pleases. In the moralistic view, the law should prescribe what is right, not merely what serves the freedom and convenience of individuals. The primary function of law is to give moral form to man's life; the function of protecting him from others is secondary. In accordance with this basic difference, the liberal must in general feel that the less law there is, the better. The moralist, on the other hand, while not necessarily totalitarian, is more open to the legal regulation of various aspects of life.

It is easy for most Americans to see the weaknesses in the moralistic view. It accords government a dangerous eminence and evinces relatively little respect for the freedom and uniqueness of personal life. The weaknesses of the liberal view, however, are not so obvious to most of us and, thus, it is particularly important to point them out. One weakness of the liberal view is that it depends on the idea that moral rules and theories are purely subjective and personal and, thus, are not things we need to be concerned with in our common life. But are not at least some rules incumbent on everyone? Presumably those against murder and theft are; and if we admit even that much we have given up the casual relativism so often expressed by liberals and have acknowledged that every human life should be carried on within a moral structure which is the same for all. It would seem also that we implicitly acknowledge a universal moral structure every time we seriously use the word "man." If the word can be accurately used, it must signify that every being who can be called "man" is in some respects the same as every other being who can be called "man." Must one not conclude that the rules of life for these beings are in some respects the same?

Another weakness in the liberal view is that it places a burden of moral understanding on the average individual that may well be too heavy for him to carry. During the last generation or two most people have come to realize that the *material* well-being of an individual is decisively affected by the whole society. An ordinary laborer in a time of severe unemployment, for example, is likely to be very poor regardless of how much initiative he has. But is not the *moral* well-being of an individual also decisively affected by society? Is not the average individual in a society that provides no moral guidance or encouragement likely to suffer the kind of confusion and discouragement which is appropriately called "demoralization"?

Finally, it may be asked whether it is possible, even if it were desirable, to place government on the periphery of moral life. It would seem that a government, through such influences as example, education, and law, inevitably has a powerful effect on the moral attitudes and practices of citizens. If so, would it not be well for political leaders, with all the wisdom they can summon, to take this effect into account in framing their words and policies?

Again, just as it was suggested that one could test his attitude toward governmental responsibility for molding belief only by imagining the most favorable possible case, here it may be suggested that one imagine a government taking steps through public education, through laws, and through the urging and example of leaders to cultivate in citizens tolerance for views they disagree with, acceptance of all races as equal, and concern for social and economic justice. Would this be objectionable?

Having reflected on the three great ends that Western man has set for government – material welfare, true belief, and the moral life – we are in a good position to ask, as the final question of this chapter, just how great a role government has in human life.

25. Should governments try to create societies that fulfill all ends and desires?

This question brings us to a vantage point overlooking one of the great chasms in the Western political mind. On one side lies what can be called "the politics of redemption." Some of the greatest thinkers in history – Plato, Rousseau, Marx – represent this general outlook. The principle defining it is simply that the end of politics, and of political thought, is a life on earth that is altogether good. There are no unconquerable evils in man or in the essential structure of earthly life. Felicity is not a gift of God, and it is not reserved for a heavenly existence or a time after death. It can be attained through human planning and can be attained here on earth. Exponents of this view are not generally bland optimists; they have often expressed deep hatred of the social and political world about them. But their mood has not been the resigned disenchantment of those who take it for granted that worldly happiness is unstable and unsatisfying. Their mood has been rather the impatience and disgust of those who feel that men have betrayed their potentialities. Finding themselves in hell, they have called for the creation of heaven. The Communist vision of a world brotherhood, arising from the conquest of all poverty, inequality, and war, exemplifies the politics of redemption.

On the other side of the chasm lies what I shall call "the politics of convenience." This may be based either on skepticism concerning the capacities of man and the possibilities of life on earth, as in many Christian thinkers, or, paradoxically, on satisfaction with things as they are. Both attitudes prompt a political mood of low expectations and low demands since the world either cannot, or need not, be much improved. Government is not expected to bring salvation but only to enhance the convenience of life. Thus, Locke, exemplifying the attitude of satisfaction with things as they are, did not assert that human life without government would be terrible or impossible. He would not dream of saying, as Rousseau did, that when man founds a government and enters into the civil state, "his faculties are so stimulated and developed, his ideas so extended, his feelings so ennobled, and his whole soul so uplifted, that, did not the abuses of this new condition often degrade him below that which he left, he would be bound to bless continually the happy moment which took him from it for ever, and, instead of a stupid and unimaginative animal, made him an intelligent being and a man." [5] That is the voice of redemptive politics. For Locke, a government may save men time and annoyance by doing for them certain things that they otherwise would have to, but could, do for themselves. But that is all; it cannot turn hell into heaven.

A chasm, not a mere line, divides these two conceptions of the

[5] Rousseau, *op. cit.*, pp. 18–19.

ends of power because each normally is attached to other concepts and attitudes to make up a whole world-view and not merely a position on one question. Those who speak for the politics of redemption are often preoccupied with the state of man's soul – for example, with his relationship to the true and good (Plato), or his moral perfection (Rousseau); those who speak for the politics of convenience are apt to be more concerned with the efficient and orderly arrangement of externals. Again, on one side all attention is given to the public realm, logically, since there can be redemption through politics only if private life is completely subordinate to public life. On the other side, what is of greatest concern is the integrity and security of the private realm, with the world beyond regarded primarily as a threat. Further, those thinkers who are engrossed in the state of the soul and the possibility of its renewal through reformation of the public world, generally view the earth as the possession of all men in common and wish either to regulate severely or to abolish private property (Plato, Rousseau, and Marx were all, in various ways and degrees, enemies of private property). On the other hand, those thinkers who are concerned mainly with the convenient arrangement of externals, and with protection of private life, are apt to be, like Locke, strong defenders of personal property.

Finally, the politics of redemption is likely to be a politics of concentrated and unlimited power. Admittedly, this is not true of Marx, for whom the final redemptive act in history, the Communist Revolution, was to prepare for the disappearance of all centralized and coercive power. But the principal practitioner of Marxism so far in history, Lenin, was an exponent of highly centralized, unconstitutional power, and both Plato and Rousseau opposed divisions and prior limitations affecting governmental power. The politics of convenience is typically expressed in ideals such as constitutionalism and the mixed state. This can be easily understood. To divide power, and draw constitutional bounds around it, is obviously prudent (unless one shares Hobbes' view of man) if one's aim is merely to eliminate some of the inconveniences of daily existence and to assure the safety of life and property. It is prudent, but it is no way to bring about "new heavens and a new earth"; if that is the aim, there must be a new political order as well.

In drawing this dichotomy, I do not mean to imply that every thinker is on one side or the other. It would be hard, for example, to know where to place Hobbes. Principally, what I want to suggest is simply that it delineates a profound and dangerous issue for Western man. Probably most Americans today are satisfied to continue with the politics of convenience which, with our vast resources and space, has served the majority fairly well. But there are strong and embittered minorities – poor people and blacks, above all – whom it has not served well. Further, it is more than doubtful that convenience, even very great convenience, enjoyed equally by all classes and races, long satisfies human beings. The "sensible" man would say that political redemption is a pipe dream and that we should be satisfied if we can just gain some convenience and comfort. Most people are not sensible, however, at least not in the long run. Nor is it obvious that they should be. From the time of Isaiah to that of Marx, men have imagined a time when "the eyes of the blind shall be opened, and the ears of the deaf shall be unstopped," when "the parched ground shall become a pool and the thirsty land springs of water." [6] Will we be nobler and better when we cease to have such thoughts? Yet into how much terror and disappointment will they lead us?

SUGGESTED READINGS

(Titles are listed chronologically. All are available in paperback or other inexpensive editions.)

Plato. *The Republic*
Aristotle. *Nicomachean Ethics*

[6] Isaiah 35:5 and 7.

Saint Augustine. *The Political Writings of St. Augustine.* Ed. by Henry Paolucci. (Regnery)
Saint Thomas Aquinas. *The Political Writings of St. Thomas Aquinas.* Ed. by Dino Bigongiari. (Hafner). Pp. 92–158
Locke, John. *A Letter Concerning Toleration*
———. *The Second Treatise of Government*
Mill, John Stuart. *On Liberty*
———. *Utilitarianism*
Green, Thomas Hill. *Lectures on the Principles of Political Obligation*
Dickinson, G. Lowes. *A Modern Symposium*
Buber, Martin. *Paths in Utopia*
Berdyaev, Nicolas. *The Destiny of Man*
Lippmann, Walter. *The Good Society*
Schumpeter, Joseph. *Capitalism, Socialism, and Democracy*
Lindsay, A. D. *The Modern Democratic State*
Niebuhr, H. Richard. *Christ and Culture*
Galbraith, John Kenneth. *The Affluent Society*
Arendt, Hannah. *The Human Condition*
———. *On Revolution*

7

The Nature and Meaning of History

A leading historian of ideas has observed that "to ask earnestly the question of the ultimate meaning of history takes one's breath away; it transports us into a vacuum which only hope and faith can fill."[1] Anyone who tries to think philosophically about history realizes immediately that this is true. All philosophical questions, simply because they arise only as inquiry is pushed to its ultimate limits, can give one the feeling of being on the edge of a precipice, but philosophical questions about history seem peculiarly abysmal. How can one possibly speak with any assurance concerning the source, the final end, and the significance of all human events?

It seems that one certainly cannot. Yet anyone who reflects on politics with seriousness and persistence is led inevitably to try. In the last analysis this is due, I think, simply to the imperfection and failure that attend all political undertakings. Even relatively modest efforts, like that of Woodrow Wilson to link the United

[1] Karl Löwith, *Meaning in History* (Chicago: University of Chicago Press, 1949), p. 4.

States with a global association of nations, are often blocked. Exalted ideals like those ascendant in France in 1789 and in Russia in 1917 usually lead to violence and tyranny. Are all great political ideals and efforts then futile? If not, which ones may bear fruit, and under what conditions? If so, why not, as Epicurus advised, forget politics and "live unknown"? When one asks such questions as these he has begun to reflect on the nature and meaning of history.

But political failure alone does not give rise to the philosophy of history. Even when the prospects of immediate success are good, we are bound to ask "What then?" unless we are so insensible as to forget that just as the present will give way to the immediate future, so that in turn will give way to the distant future. If world peace and perfect justice are achieved, what then? The answer is that the person who asks the question and all of his contemporaries will die. Any paradise they create will be left to strange generations. Finally, too, any paradise they create will decay and the earth itself will become uninhabitable. Many people can ignore these certainties, but there is no way in which, with philosophical good conscience, we can deny them or suppress the sense of ultimate pointlessness that arises from them.

Let us begin with one of the more manageable questions concerning history, a question that everyday politics must in one way or another force to the attention of even practical-minded persons when they consider how seldom the ends of governments are fully achieved.

26. What determines the course of history?

Several modern thinkers have clearly assumed, without explicitly stating, the answer most of us want to hear: that man – no impersonal force, and no god – determines the course of history. Rousseau is a good example. His condemnation of eighteenth-century civilization, and his eloquent descriptions of the new society which lived in his imagination, the depth of his exasperation, and the height of his hope, are inexplicable apart from the assumption that man can, if he wills to, establish a new order and, thus, alter the course of history. Moreover, as we noted in discussing the concept of original sin, Rousseau believed man was free so to will. He has not, contrary to Augustine, lost his original innocence. It is true that he has become tragically entangled in historical circumstances, such as inequitable systems of property ownership, and these have diverted his will from its true end. But he could extricate himself if he determined to do so. Rousseau began the first chapter of *The Social Contract* with the famous words, "Man is born free, and everywhere he is in chains." The book as a whole is an effort to show that the chains can be broken.

For Rousseau, the pure human will which can set a new direction for history is the will of the people. Others who believe that the human will can control events embrace what is often called "the great man theory of history." According to this view the dominant will must be that of a hero, such as Alexander the Great or Lenin.

But probably the most widespread form at present of the confidence that human beings are potential sovereigns of history does not rely on will at all but on knowledge. Science, rather than the uncorrupted will either of the people or of heroes, will enable us to attain our ends. An idea of this sort is at least in the back of the minds of many social scientists today. Among the great thinkers, it was explicitly argued by John Stuart Mill (1806–1873). In a book which is not read very much today but was widely studied in the Victorian age, *A System of Logic,* Mill expressed confidence that an authentic and all-inclusive science of society could be perfected. Government would then be based on empirically tested knowledge rather than on political guesswork. Mill did not think science could make possible the prediction and control of every detail in history, but it could provide reliable guidance for those in a position to take unpredictable details into account. The general ideal he sketched was that of history made comprehensible and controllable by scientific knowledge.

The idea that we can will, or scientifically plan, a new historical era reflects the hopeful, man-centered attitude of the modern world and has helped to inspire both the revolutions that have punctuated European history since 1789 and the intense activity that has peopled and industrialized the North American continent.

In view of the power of this idea, it is somewhat surprising that the oldest and deepest tendency of the Western mind is in the opposite direction toward the idea that the course of history is determined by something other than the will or knowledge of man. Ancient thought, despite its intense concern with man and its confidence in the potential sweep and power of his knowledge, was conspicuously lacking in the historical self-assurance of modern man. The sense of a fate that spells uncertainty for all plans and mortality for all societies was strong. Plato believed that even the government of philosophers was doomed finally to decay owing to the imperfection of their knowledge. As for Christianity, the orthodox conception of history was one of divine determinism. The life of Jesus was seen as the enactment and disclosure of God's historical intent. Man might respond, or fail to respond, but he could not alter the effect of divine decrees.

It is an indication of the hold of such determinism on our minds that it should reappear in the modern world in the thought of the most worldly and revolutionary of men, the Communists. In Marxist philosophy divine determinism is replaced by economic determinism. The general course of history is determined by laws of economic development as irresistible in the Communist view as the divine plan of salvation in the minds of Christians. Of course, the laws of economic development are believed to result from human, not divine, activity, and as capitalist society matures and the proletarian revolution approaches, the grip of these laws on human behavior is loosened and there is increasing scope for human will and knowledge. Yet for Marx as definitely as for Augustine, history unfolds according to a pattern man has not designed and cannot significantly vary.

No small part of the demoralization of the present time is due to the fact that we do not know what to think about these matters. Since the beginning of World War I in 1914, a series of profound and unforeseen disasters has shaken our confidence. After a half-century that has included two prolonged and ruinous world wars, a protracted economic depression, the tyrannies of Hitler and Stalin, with their calculated and extravagant violations of human dignity, and a dangerous and apparently endless "Cold War," we doubt that history is under the direction either of man or of any other beneficent force. Such a feeling of historical estrangement might be fairly easily borne by a religious civilization, for faith in things beyond history would remain. But modern men have counted far less in rising above history than on dominating it, and less on entering another world than on perfecting the one we now inhabit. In these circumstances, to lose confidence in the future is to suffer a basic spiritual disorientation.

In order to reflect on the entire problem, however, it is necessary to ask a second question. The modern sense that history is meaningful and benign has come from two sources: confidence in man's ability to control historical events and also the sense that there is a natural tendency – working perhaps even without deliberate human control – for the conditions and quality of life to improve. In short, we have relied not only on human power but also on spontaneous progress. We no longer trust the latter any more than we do the former. Hence, having asked what determines the movement of history, we must now ask concerning the direction of this movement.

27. Does history lead naturally toward a better earthly life for men?

For some generations modern man has answered with an exuberant "Yes." Progress has been taken to be a natural, if not inevitable, characteristic of human history. A typical and influential representative of this view is Antoine-Nicolas de Condorcet (1743–1794). The core idea in Condorcet's philosophy of history is the limitless perfectibility of man. But in maintaining this principle Condorcet meant not only that man *may* become perfect, which Rousseau, an opponent of the doctrine of progress, also believed, he meant that man has a strong bent toward perfection. This is the source of progress. It comes about principally through rational enlightenment. Science deepens knowledge, printing and education spread it. It is assumed in Socratic fashion that growth in knowledge must be accompanied by growth in moral excellence. Condorcet admitted that the course of progress might be interrupted. His rationalism was coupled with a deep hostility toward religion, and he looked back on the Middle Ages as a time of superstition, intolerance, and priestly oppression. But he seems to have had little fear that man might descend forever into some era of darkness. He saw the human race moved by a nearly irresistible destiny toward enlightenment, and through enlightenment toward universal freedom and equality.

Among other well-known exponents of progress in recent times are Hegel and Marx. One can see in both thinkers the strength of the modern inclination to believe in progress regardless of what the determining force of history is thought to be. Neither attributed preponderant influence to conscious will or to knowledge. For one ideas, for the other economic laws, ordered the march of affairs. At some points, they assumed, these had to be known and consciously acted upon, but for long periods they might shape the outcome of events despite the resistance and ignorance of participants. In the long run, they thought progress inevitable. The inadequacies of men might delay it but never could completely block it.

The authority of the idea of progress is particularly evident in the Hegelian and Marxist "dialectic." Both thinkers believed that history moves, so to speak, in a "zig-zag" fashion rather than in a straight line. Progress is not a steady and harmonious forward movement, but comes about through tension and conflict, and the most catastrophic moments may presage the most glorious ones. This is to say that human beings are often wrong-headed and often stand against the forward march of history. Far from inhibiting progress, however, error and conflict are among the devices by which progress is accomplished. Assurance of the ascendant course of history could hardly be more emphatically affirmed.

However, just as we had to point out above that belief in man's power to direct history is more than counterbalanced by the older and more enduring conviction that history is determined by some power beyond man, so here it is necessary to make it clear that the doctrine of progress, although very popular during the last century or two, is far from expressing the consensus of Western thinkers. On the contrary, the history of thought reflects a great deal of pessimism about the spontaneous course of events. The ancient Greeks and Romans generally assumed that history moves through more or less regular cycles; recurrence, rather than progress, was seen as the law of history. It is easy to understand how such an idea might arise. Recurrence is a pronounced and even awesome characteristic of man's environment and life. For example, it occurs in the changing of the seasons and the passing of the generations. But while the idea of historical cycles is in this sense comprehensible, it expresses a mood very far from the hopefulness of Condorcet and other apostles of progress. If history is cyclical, then ultimately nothing is accomplished. There may be achievements within a single cycle, but the long ages of history, including many cycles, can be nothing more than the recurrent decay and restoration of what was achieved in the first cycle. A terrible futility reigns in human affairs.

Augustine and other Christian thinkers repudiated the cyclical conception of history. They had to. Otherwise the life of Christ, as well as all other actions of God, would have fallen under the law and been cursed by the absurdity of endless repetition. However the alternative view developed by Christian thinkers was also markedly pessimistic. History was envisioned as leading toward a finale of suffering and terror: "For nation shall rise against nation, and kingdom against kingdom: and there shall be earthquakes in divers places, and there shall be famines and troubles." [2] With the end of history, of course, God was finally to establish His Kingdom, and this climax, to which all of the ages since Adam's sin had been leading, would give history a meaning such as it could not have if it were governed by the law of cyclical recurrence. In this sense history leads toward a better life for men. But not toward a better *earthly* life. God's Kingdom was thought to be, in its perfection, completely unlike any historical kingdom. Nothing perfect or lasting can be created in history, which began with man's rebellion against God and is destined to end catastrophically. It is plain that while history has a purpose and meaning in the Christian vision which it cannot have in classical conceptions, there is an immense chasm between the Christian vision and the modern idea of progress. In the former, the beginning is sin; in the latter, it is innocence. In the former, the dominant motif is tragedy; in the latter, steady improvement. Christians expected "affliction, such as was not from the beginning of the creation which God created unto this time," [3] while Condorcet and his followers looked for increasing harmony and happiness on this earth.

Today, we do not know what to think about the natural course of history any more than we do about the question of what determines it. And our doubts in the one case, as in the other, are owing to the unexpected disasters that have befallen mankind since 1914. The idea of progress has suddenly come to seem old-fashioned and unrealistic. But what can we put in place of it? We do not have enough religious faith to return to the Christian idea that history ends with the destruction of the world and the establishment of a heavenly kingdom, although many sense an apocalyptic quality in the nuclear cloud. The cyclical conception

[2] Mark 13:8.
[3] Mark 13:19.

of history seems implausible too, and intolerable as well. It is implausible because for two millennia, under both Christianity and secular progressivism, men have been taught that history has a direction and a purpose. Further, in the last two centuries, we have seen events like industrialization which we know have never happened before and which thus seem to disprove any theory of cyclical recurrence. Such a view is intolerable because, after believing for so long that history is purposeful, we are crushed by the thought that it is merely endless, useless repetition.

In James Joyce's novel *Ulysses* one of the characters says that history is a nightmare from which he is trying to awake.[4] This remark expresses the mood of historical insecurity and fear that has been created in many people today by half a century of disorder and violence. It expresses the mood that must descend on men who have confidence neither in their own control of history nor in the beneficence of its natural tendencies. If we can neither control nor trust the course of events, it is difficult not to feel that the universe is a capricious despot who may, at any time, wreck our relationships and our lives. Personal existence is burdened by the impression that the surrounding universe is senseless and fearful. Political life is demoralized by the sense that the consequences of any program of action are incalculable and menacing.

But are one's relationships with other men and with the universe totally subject to history? Is there not a changeless structure of right and truth which a moral and rational being can inhabit regardless of the uncertainty and destructiveness of history? It would be reassuring to think that there is, that certain standards and truths, at least, are not engulfed in history. A number of thinkers, however, would deny even this reassurance. All realities, all principles, all moral rules are mutable. Thus everything is submerged in the flow of events, and the futility and tragedy of history encompass the whole world in which man lives. Is this true?

[4] James Joyce, *Ulysses* (New York: The Modern Library, 1914), p. 35.

28. Do the basic principles of reality and right change in the course of history?

The notion that they do is bound to be disturbing to anyone who fully understands it and sees that this idea may, indeed, be valid. Students often lightly assert that what is true and good for one era may not be so for another. But often, perhaps, they do not fully realize what they are saying, for if they are right, there are no fixed points in relation to which one's life can be guided. One who comes to perceive the universe in this way finds that all standards are upset. Liberty, democracy, justice, respect for life, honesty – every rule one might rely on for conducting his life and appraising his surroundings gives way. And not only right and wrong, but reality itself, dissolves and is carried away in the flux of events. One cannot hold to "human nature" or to any other rock. Indeed, if one takes with full seriousness the idea that all basic principles change in the course of history he must find even that idea escaping like water through his fingers, for it too must be one of those principles that changes as history moves.

The contemporary French writer and thinker, Jean-Paul Sartre, has written a novel entitled *Nausea.* In this book he depicts with great dramatic force the vertigo and horror felt by a man who sees reality as completely lacking in firm structure and meaning. Nothing, not even one's hand, has any clear form or purpose. In this kind of molten, meaningless universe one can only feel nausea.

Thus it is not surprising that men have always tried to find ground above the flood of change and that political thinkers have sought principles of human relations that will not crumble and disappear in the stream of history. Indeed, it is hardly too much to say that political philosophy began with an effort to find firm ground. Plato as a young man saw the dissolution not only of Athenian political institutions but also of Hellenic moral and religious convictions. Athenian governments were repeatedly overthrown and there were men everywhere who said, and acted as though they believed, that there were no fixed standards of right. Plato must have felt that all of the constituents of civilization were being dissolved. Accordingly, the major premise of *The Republic* is that a good state can be founded only on an understanding of what is always true and always good. Plato's famous doctrine of forms represented an effort to say what this is. In the framework of this doctrine, every real entity – every man, tree, chair, or rock – is real only because it participates in a universal, changeless form – the form of a man, a tree, a chair, or a rock. These forms, for Plato, were what we might call "ideas," or "essences." They could not be seen or touched but could only be known intellectually. Above all, they *are* and do not come into being or pass away; they have no history. The concept of "the Good," which we have already discussed, entered into this doctrine. "The Good" may be thought of as the form of all forms, the eternal source of all being. The philosopher was envisioned by Plato as one who has ascended from things that are seen and touched to the world of forms, and from the forms to the Good. This is to say that he had ascended from the changing to the lasting. Only when philosophers gain absolute power can a just state be founded and the confusion and violence of historical life be ended. This is the main theme of *The Republic.* Plato's aim was to found statecraft on principles unaffected by history.

The general view set forth in *The Republic* is not unique, however, and was not novel even in Plato's time. Plato simply took up a search which had already been initiated by other philosophers and has continued to our own day, a search for what is most commonly called "nature." I have already briefly discussed the ancient issue of nature *versus* convention. One of the most notable features of this controversy is that convention has had so few defenders. The idea of nature for millennia has had a remarkable, only occasionally questioned, authority. One of the principal reasons for this seems to be that nature, the basic structure of being, does not change, or, at least, so it has been conceived. The idea of natural law, of a set of moral imperatives that reason can discern in nature, is probably the most durable and powerful idea in the whole history of Western moral and political thought. What the idea consists in essentially is the proposition that there is a law of human relations that is above history. Times and customs may change but the principles governing the relations of one person to another remain the same. Many of our most civilized institutions, such as personal liberties, popular government, and international law and organization, can be traced back to this idea. If this one timber in the structure of our civilization were suddenly withdrawn we might find ourselves standing in the midst of ruins.

Even the ancient Hebrews, with their profound historical consciousness, sought a standpoint above the flux of history. The Hebrews did not share the typical Greek belief in a permanent order of nature. Even Jehovah (or perhaps one should say *particularly* Jehovah) was beyond any knowable order, could make free, unforeseeable decisions, and could even repent of things He had done. But "the mercy of the Lord is from everlasting to everlasting," and one of the acts of this mercy was the gift of a set of laws, ten master principles of human relations which, as divine commandments, were impervious to historical erosion.

The quest for inalterable realities and rules has been pressed so persistently that one feels in it the expression of a basic imperative of human existence. It seems that we can hardly live if nothing endures. Nevertheless, the last two centuries have seen numerous attacks on "nature" and natural law. As for the former (what is, as distinguished from what ought to be) some of the most profound and persuasive philosophers have argued against the notion that there is a knowable, inalterable structure of being. Hume did so in maintaining the thesis that no necessary connection links cause and effect. When we speak of these, according to Hume, we merely report recurrent sequences in our sensations. We have no right to make assertions concerning the basic order of things, and we cannot know that there is such an order. A similar view was put forward by Kant, in spite of his intention of refuting Hume. One of the main themes of *The Critique of Pure Reason* is that the changeless structure men thought they had discovered is imposed by the mind and does not hold among the "things-in-themselves." The idea of a changeless natural order was challenged from another angle by Henri Bergson (1859–1941), whose popularity has declined somewhat but who was a thinker of great originality and eloquence. According to Bergson, the essence of the real is change. "There do not exist *things* made, but only things in the making, not *states* that remain fixed, but only states in process of change."[5] This is most obvious in the case of life and of man. Bergson admitted that some realities are relatively fixed, but these are dead and inorganic, not alive and spiritual. The quest for the changeless he condemned as an effort to impose the fixity which is alone suited to our intellects on what is intrinsically "unceasing creation."[6] As a final example of the modern rejection of structure, note may be taken of existentialism. Perhaps the single common theme uniting all varieties of existentialism is the denial that human nature is a changeless, transhistorical form. Man is free, or subjective, and thus beyond every fixed, objective principle.

So far as views of this sort prevail, the belief in changeless moral principles tends to decline. Kant showed, to be sure, that this is not an invariable rule; he set forth a moral theory that has become almost notorious in its rigid and uncompromising conception of duty. But the traditional idea of natural law necessarily falls if there is no nature. Hume founded morality on the wants and propensities of the individual, as well as on custom and habit; for Bergson, a good act was a creative act, one arising from an intuitive sense of the movement of life; existentialists have typically argued that choice is not subordinated to values but rather that it creates values. None of these thinkers would have said that anything is good because an individual or a society calls it good. They were not total relativists. But all reflect the

[5] Henri Bergson, *The Creative Mind: An Introduction to Metaphysics* (New York: Philosophical Library, 1946), p. 188. The italics are Bergson's.
[6] *Ibid.*, p. 18.

decay of the ancient conviction that certain principles of right remain despite all historical change. And all reflect the rise of the relativism that pervades American academic life, particularly in the social sciences.

A good example of the prevalent view that all right is relative to time and place is the thought of Marx. Much of the force of Marx's writing lay in the apparent demonstration that many realities and standards which had been regarded as part of the inalterable order of nature, such as the profit motive, private property, and government by parliaments, were in actuality merely the beliefs and customs of a particular historical era and destined to disappear. Marx as a man was not without absolute moral standards, as is plain in his bitter denunciations of the capitalist system. As a thinker, however, he had no such standards. His aim was not to show that capitalist civilization was evil but that it was temporary. His revolutionary power is due to the skill and thoroughness with which he swept all aspects of the civilization he hated into the torrent of history.

Is it merely a sign of weakness in man that for so many centuries he tried to ground society on the changeless – on eternal "forms," on "nature," or on God? Or is it due to an intuition that relationships without such a foundation can have no substance or validity? With questions like these we are groping our way among the shadows of contemporary despair. We have little confidence in the course of history, and we are afraid that our being and relationships are wholly at the mercy of whatever erratic or catastrophic turn history may take. These anxieties give rise to the final question of this book: Can an individual stand aside and create a life for himself alone, apart from history?

29. Can one escape from history?

This is one of the most critical questions of our time, not so much for the civilization as a whole as for each one individually. Our historical troubles are profound: war, racial conflict, disintegrating cities, pollution of water and air. Anyone living now can be sure that his whole life will be carried on amid the kind of large-scale turmoil and affliction that will be described by historians even into the distant future. Is all personal happiness then doomed? Or might one who uses his wits shield himself from these surrounding adversities and live well despite them?

Ours is not the first age to ask such questions. We have already mentioned the period after Philip of Macedon and his son Alexander the Great had shown at the Battle of Chaeronea (338 B.C.) that the city-state was anachronistic. The passing of the city-state was, in the words of a leading historian of political theory. George Sabine, a "major moral disaster." [7] The city-state had been widely regarded as the only possible framework for a good life, and it was suddenly swept into the past. This, as Sabine puts it, "forced upon men the creation for the first time of ideals of personal character and private happiness." [8] Philosophers of various persuasions – Cynics, Stoics, Epicureans – began to call on the individual to achieve that quality which formerly had been demanded only of the city-state: self-sufficiency. It is possible for an individual to live with dignity and composure regardless of the disorder, or the impersonal and alien order, like that established by Macedon and Rome, in the world around him. In short, it is possible to escape from history.

There were two main conceptions of this possibility. For Cynics and early Stoics the escape from history could be accomplished through a contemptuous disregard of established conventions and through practice of a severe and proud morality. For Epicureans it depended on avoiding political entanglements and on minimizing the pain of daily life. The crucial differences between these two conceptions of withdrawal is that in effect they rested on different answers to the preceding question of whether there is

[7] George H. Sabine, *A History of Political Theory*, third edition (New York: Holt, Rinehart and Winston, 1961), p. 130.
[8] *Ibid.*, p. 131.

a changeless structure of reality and right beyond history. Cynics and Stoics held that there was. The wise man was the inhabitant of a cosmic order unrelated to worldly history. He could live in this order and be completely untouched by historical turmoil. Epicureans, in contrast, relied on no cosmic structure. For them, consequently, escape from history was an act of purely personal defiance and self-seclusion. The individual did not withdraw into an eternal order but into a realm of privacy which he himself had to create and sustain.

In modern times such views have been reiterated, although the motive for doing so has been not so much despair of history as disinterest. Liberals of a certain kind have pictured the life of mankind as a multitude of unique and separate lives, as though each individual carried on his existence within a private compartment. They have generally acknowledged that the security and separateness of the individual's life depend on certain conditions in the surrounding world, such as lawful government. But they have held that these conditions are not numerous and that so long as they prevail one can and should live in his own way, regardless of how others may live, regardless, that is, of history. Thus, it is hardly too much to say that Locke's political theory was an effort to define those arrangements that are necessary if the individual is to live his own unique and separate life, apart from his times.

Locke wrote in the seventeenth century. In the nineteenth century another great English liberal, John Stuart Mill voiced the ideal of a unique and separate life in a way that was very reminiscent of Locke. Mill distinguished between "self-regarding" and "other-regarding" acts. The former are acts with direct and important consequences only for oneself; the latter have substantial effects on others. The striking thing about this apparently sensible distinction is the underlying assumption, without which the distinction would be trivial, that the sphere of self-regarding acts is large and important. Much that is of serious concern to each individual is assumed to be of no serious concern to anyone else. As examples of those matters that belong altogether within one's private compartment, Mill suggests thoughts, feelings, and opinions, as well as "tastes and pursuits."[9] It was Mill's aim, moreover, not only to assert the possibility of separate individual life but to set forth its glory. The essay *On Liberty* may be read as a call to each one to carry out his own heroic escape from history.

In asking whether one *can* escape from history we have in effect asked both whether it would be actually *possible* and whether it would be morally *permissible.* Thinkers who have dealt with this question have not carefully made this distinction and it seems unnecessary that we do so in this discussion. It may be noted, however, that those who have asserted that one can escape from history have in general dwelt upon the moral desirability of such an act. On the other hand, those who have asserted one cannot escape from history have stressed the practical impossibility of doing so. Let us then call the affirmative side that of "individuality" and the negative side that of "interdependence."

The idea of interdependence is far older and more common than that of individuality. Aristotle's conception of man as a "political animal" was in part the conception that human beings are in everything – feelings, opinions, and ways of life – thoroughly interdependent. (The question of whether one can escape from history is not the same as the first question of this book: Are men united in essence? One might, like the early Stoics, answer that they are united in essence but are not, in fact, interdependent and that their essential unity is realized only in an eternal order beyond history. One might assert that history is a level of existence in which men are estranged and their essential unity violated. One would then be compelled to withdraw from history in order to join with men.) Aristotle's view was common among Greeks in the city-state era. The thought of the Middle Ages too, despite the spirit of individuality inherent in the

[9] John Stuart Mill, *Utilitarianism, Liberty, and Representative Government* (New York: E. P. Dutton, 1951), p. 99.

Christian idea that God saves individuals and not groups, was filled with organic conceptions of human relations. John of Salisbury, who is known as a typical voice of the medieval political mind, wrote a long treatise on politics based on the idea that the structure of society is analogous in all major features to the structure of the human body.

In modern times the most influential exponent of interdependence probably has been Karl Marx. The theory of Marx was a total repudiation of the businessman's notion, derived from the thought of Locke, that an individual's economic circumstances depend on himself and not on society. The material fate of each man, according to Marx, depends on his situation in history. Moreover, the "economic determinism" we have already discussed meant that on his material fate, in turn, depend his feelings and ideas, his "tastes and pursuits." Thus both the physical and spiritual condition of a person are historically determined. Some of the overpowering force of the Marxist resolution that history shall be transformed is undoubtedly due to the conviction that history is inescapable.

During the time Marx was writing, a similar conviction was expressed by a great American leader who was living through one of the great historical tragedies of modern times, the American Civil War. "Fellow-citizens," members of Congress were told by Abraham Lincoln, "we cannot escape history. We of this Congress and this administration will be remembered in spite of ourselves. No personal significance or insignificance can spare one or another of us. The fiery trial through which we pass will light us down, in honor or dishonor, to the latest generation." [10]

In his symbolic novel, *The Plague,* Albert Camus depicted the obsession, on the part of some, with escaping from a quarantined, disease-ridden city. It was difficult to escape, but not impossible, and the lives of a few were dedicated to that single end.

[10] Abraham Lincoln, "Annual Message to Congress, 1862," in *The Life and Writings of Abraham Lincoln,* ed. by Philip Van Doren Stern (New York: The Modern Library, 1940), p. 745.

Likewise, if we could escape from our own bewildering and oppressive times – from the plagues of racial conflict, urban disintegration, and international war – this possibility would stand out for some as the single, existing avenue toward life and happiness.

But if man cannot escape from history, then the paths of thought we have been following, and which have now led us entirely across the area of political thought, have brought us to a boundary we cannot traverse. They have brought us, as it were, to sheer cliffs and we must remain in the territory we have explored. If we are condemned to live in history then we are condemned also to think about politics, for to do this is simply to think about how we should carry on our lives in common.

SUGGESTED READINGS

(Titles are listed chronologically. All are available in paperback or other inexpensive editions.)

Saint Augustine. *The City of God*
Hegel, Georg Wilhelm Friedrich. *The Philosophy of History*
Marx, Karl, and Engels, Friedrich. *The Communist Manifesto*
Mill, John Stuart. *On Liberty*
Bergson, Henri. *The Two Sources of Morality and Religion*
Bury, J. B. *The Ideas of Progress*
Berdyaev, Nicholas. *The Meaning of History*
Niebuhr, Reinhold. *The Nature and Destiny of Man,* Vol. 2
Popper, Karl. *The Open Society and Its Enemies,* 2 vols.
Löwith, Karl. *Meaning in History*
Niebuhr, Reinhold. *The Irony of American History*
Frankel, Charles. *The Case for Modern Man*
Bultmann, Rudolf. *History and Eschatology: The Presence of Eternity*

Epilogue
The Idea of Humane Uncertainty

How can one keep from intellectual despair in the face of questions which have for twenty-five centuries defied the efforts of philosophers to find demonstrable, universally acceptable answers? To show that there are perennial questions about politics may serve to rebut heedless votaries of religious dogma or of science who assume that no great questions remain unanswered. However, it may only fortify those who shun political speculation not because they assume the great questions have already been answered but because they assume they can never be answered.

Consequently, it may be in order to remind readers who have taken the trouble to consider the questions in this book of two points suggested in the introductory chapter.

The first is that answers are possible. They cannot be established with the objective certainty of scientific laws. The failure of political thinkers to reach agreement in twenty-five centuries of speculation shows that this is so. But the history of thought is not completely discouraging, for it shows that men repeatedly overcome their uncertainties and take positions with assurance.

How can this be done? How is it possible for an intelligent person to take with assurance a philosophical position which he knows is not objectively certain? This is a mysterious spiritual event and it would not be feasible in a book of this kind to try fully to explain it. A few suggestions, however, may be in order. It seems that a philosophical idea is the symbol of an inner state that is something different from and independent of the idea. Plato's concept of the philosopher-king, for example, symbolized a vision of men at one with the source of being and with other men. One gains only the slightest glimmering of this vision merely by comprehending and joining the words "philosopher" and "king." The idea and the vision are two different entities. If this is so, the idea may be objectively uncertain yet the vision, the inner state, may feel unshakable and certain. This equivocal state of mind enables one to enter into authentic inquiry, exposing his basic beliefs to examination and doubt, without jeopardizing the very spiritual foundations of his life. It is the only possible basis of toleration. Those for whom ideas and inner state are identical can be tolerant, in a settled and open way, only if they are complete skeptics. Once they adopt any ideas, then their whole vision of themselves and the universe is at stake whenever their ideas are challenged, and they cannot afford, as a settled policy, to leave themselves exposed to such an ordeal. Thus dogmatic Christians who thought God's mind and intent were exactly expressed in the words and phrases of the orthodox creed were bound to try to suppress those who doubted it. They could not admit any "perennial questions" because for them inquiry and vision, doubt and inner assurance, were incompatible.

We suggest that they are not incompatible. Man needs to inquire, endlessly, but also to understand. He needs to confront those questions that must occur to civilized societies in every generation and to mature individuals at every age, and at the same time he needs to achieve inner composure. The history of thought and faith shows that men can gain the spiritual balance for doing both.

The second point that may be appropriately reiterated, in view of the apparent hopelessness of answering definitively the great questions of political thought, is that much of the value of thinking lies in thinking itself. It was suggested in the opening chapter that this is because thinking cultivates a kind of awareness. In thinking a person becomes aware of himself as a being who can stand aside and question the surrounding world and society; he becomes aware of the experiences and convictions that constitute his own particular identity, and he becomes aware of others as beings who also are able to ask questions and thus are potential companions in inquiry. Where few principles are known, as in the very early stages of human development, a great deal of reality must remain in darkness. On the other hand, where many principles are known, but with little sense of their incompleteness, of their uncertainty, and of the fact that a principle is not the same thing as the reality it symbolizes, then some of the most important realities, such as persons, with their capacity for asking questions and choosing between alternatives, and thus for diverging from all predictions and intellectual formulations, are frozen in an icy, uncomprehending certitude. This has often happened among religious believers and among devotees of science (although neither religion nor science of necessity entails such dogmatism). Only through thinking, in which principles are known but are also subject to being questioned and changed, do we enter into full awareness of our humanity.

This awareness is not without political meaning. For one thing, from awareness of my own power of asking questions arises an intuition that any organization or authority that attempts to suppress my questions and to make me a mere thoughtless and automatic part of some monolithic group, like a totalitarian state, violates my essential being. Further, the experience of questioning carries an intuition not only of freedom but also of equality. One person may know more about mathematics, or automobile engines, or history, than another, but before the perennial questions we are all, in our lack of definite, demonstrable answers, equal. The wise stand above others only in their consciousness of this primal equality.

I suggest, in sum, that wisdom is not gained by answering questions in a way that leaves them forever behind but in establishing a thoughtful and continuing relationship to questions. Wisdom is a thinking state.

This point of view is inspired and exemplified by a great historical figure, Socrates – the ugly, amiable, and devastatingly intelligent Athenian who finally suffered a judicial penalty of death as a result of questioning the young men and leaders of Athens so persistently and penetratingly that the reputations of public men and the very stability of the government seemed to be threatened. Apparently Socrates did not expound a complete and definite doctrine but concentrated instead on asking questions about such matters as courage and friendship and justice. He devoted his whole mature life to the discussion of these questions. Although he was particularly interested in talking with men who had reputations for wisdom, apparently he gladly entered into discourse with any willing participant he happened to encounter in the gymnasiums or other public places in Athens. He concluded at the end of his life that no one could answer his questions and that those who were reputed to be wise were in reality ignorant.

Two points are particularly notable, however, in relation to the ideal of "humane uncertainty" that we are sketching. The first is that Socrates concluded not only that all others were ignorant but that he himself was ignorant. He was superior to others, he held, only in his awareness of his ignorance. A lifetime of questioning had led him to no answers. It had led him only to a point at which he was so hated and mistrusted by his fellow Athenians that they condemned him to death for introducing spiritual and intellectual confusion into the city.[1]

The second notable point is that Socrates lived the last days

[1] The charges against him were introducing novel religious practices and corrupting the youth.

of a life which had brought him to complete intellectual uncertainty and a shameful death with supreme composure, as though his life's effort had magnificently succeeded. At his trial, his defense was characterized, as his conversation always had been, by a good-natured but disconcerting irony. In prison, he refused to save his life by escaping because of a voice murmuring in his ears, "like the sound of the flute in the ears of the mystic," that told him he would thus betray the laws under which he had always lived. He devoted his final hours to discussing the question of whether there is life after death, and, according to Plato, during the final moments of his life, after "readily and cheerfully" drinking the hemlock, he calmed his weeping friends.[2] Socrates did not act like a man who had been reduced, by thinking, to a state of total perplexity. His ignorance seemed to be the paradoxical sign of an awareness that was inexpressible but so powerful and all-encompassing that even the imminence of death did not affect his tranquillity.

We have no certain knowledge of Socrates' political outlook. He was probably as unwilling to identify himself with definite political principles as he was with principles of any other kind. But it is not difficult to see certain broad political ideals exemplified in his life. To begin with, his whole career was a moving enactment of freedom. He was ridiculed by his fellow-citizens and threatened with exile and death by his government, but imperturbably continued to live and to speak according to the imperatives of his own being. Further, although Socrates may have had elitist leanings, such as those manifest in the idea of the philosopher-king, enunciated by his follower Plato, his manner of life suggests a certain egalitarianism. He claimed no special authority for himself and was apparently willing to talk with anyone who was willing to talk with him. In one of the Platonic dialogues he is depicted as demonstrating that significant knowledge can be elicited from an uneducated young slave. Finally,

[2] These events are recounted in three works by Plato: the *Apology*, the *Crito*, and the *Phaedo*.

he was a thoroughly communal man. Loyalty to the very city-state that sentenced him to death kept him from escaping, and his stubborn questioning represented an indefeasible openness to communication.

For most of us, doubt is unsettling, and we evade serious discussion because we are afraid of doubt. Socrates seems to say that doubt is a source of health and hope, and that the confidence of a free and communal man is born, strangely, of uncertainty.

We are living today in a period of uncertainty, but it is an anxious and debilitating uncertainty, not the serene and luminous uncertainty of Socrates. As brought out in connection with one of the questions above, not only traditional religious faith, but even the assurance that science is illuminating reality, is weak. Vast multitudes of people crowding the earth have no clear and stable ideas about what is real or how they ought to live. The spiritual situation could hardly be more ominous.

If the idea of humane uncertainty is valid, however, this situation is not hopeless, and we should not try totally to eradicate our doubts. They may be a pathway to deeper insights than any to which mankind yet has attained. When we try to substitute for our doubts objective principles that cannot be shaken or destroyed, we refuse out of fear to follow this pathway. And we may in this way do something worse than fail to deepen our understanding. The totalitarianism and violence of our time are due in some measure to the efforts of men to escape from uncertainty. Those who cannot live with doubt cannot live with human beings who are thoughtful and independent enough to be sources of doubt. Thus, for the sake both of understanding and of community, we may hope that our age of anxious uncertainty does not give way to one of perfect certainty. The greatest achievement of political thinking today would not be to overcome our doubts but to help us live with them in a state of freedom and civility.

Appendix: How to Think—Some Suggestions

The first thing a student must be taught about thinking is simply that it is unteachable. Much is said about "teaching students to think." But all a teacher can do is to offer encouragement and criticism. There are few procedures and techniques to be taught. The appearance of an idea is a mysterious occurrence, and it is doubtful that anyone does, or ever will, understand just how it comes about.

But this is not to say a student cannot *learn* to think. The reason for saying he cannot be *taught* is to focus at the outset on the fact that everything depends on the student's own solitary efforts. It is both the glory and the burden of thought that it is an exceedingly personal undertaking. The solitude of the mature thinker must be entered into immediately by the merest beginner. As the former thinks all alone, the latter must *learn* to think all alone. Occasionally one may receive a gift of encouragement or useful criticism, but nothing is decided by these. What everything depends on is the capacity for solitary effort.

It follows that little can be offered here beyond some fragmentary suggestions.

1. Do not try to arrive at ideas that no one has ever thought of before. Not many of even the greatest thinkers have done that. The aim of thinking is to discover the ideas which make one whole and the world comprehensible, not to give birth to unprecedented conceptions. An idea is your own if it has grown by your own efforts and is rooted in your own emotions and experience, even though you may have borrowed the seeds from another source, and even though the idea may be very much like ideas held by many others.

2. Be open. Ideas cannot be deliberately produced like industrial products. They appear uncommanded, they "occur," as we recognize when we say, "It occurred to me that . . . ." Hence one places himself in a fundamentally wrong relationship to ideas if he thinks of himself as controlling their appearance. He can only be open to them.

3. Do not hurry. Initial efforts to think about a problem are often completely frustrating. They may best be regarded as a tilling of the ground. Time is required before anything can be expected to grow.

4. Make plenty of notes. It is easier to do work with your mind if you are doing some corresponding work with your hands. It is often helpful to make notes on large pads where there is room for sketching out patterns of ideas. It can also be helpful to make notes on cards in a way that facilitates the cutting up of the card so that each idea noted is on a small section of card. These then can be laid out on a desk and rearranged. Often this process suggests new connections.

5. Finally, I offer what may seem like a strange injunction to offer in a textbook: Beware of too much reading. Reading about the thoughts of others is not at all the same as having thoughts of your own. To be sure, one who engages in thinking needs some acquaintance with the thoughts of others. The great thinkers inspire, provoke, confirm, and in other ways help one to do his own thinking. Nevertheless, in order to think one must at some point lay down the book and take on the labor of moving

forward with his own ideas alone. The danger of reading lies in the fact that it is easier than thinking and thus tempts one to substitute reading for thinking. In doing this one can gain the illusion that he is not only thinking but that he is doing so on a higher level than the great thinkers, since he is able to look down upon and criticize their thoughts. The study of the thoughts of others is a worthy intellectual discipline but a very different discipline than that of framing thoughts of your own. The common failure to make this distinction in academic life has been very destructive of thought.

How can one know whether an idea that has occurred to him, and that he has shaped and polished, is true? There are some standard and well-known tests: it must be consistent with other ideas one holds at the same time; and it should explain, or at the very least be compatible with, all established, relevant facts. But a merely formal, dispassionate application of these criteria does not carry one very far. They never lead, in the field of political theory, to proof. Nor do they lead to life. A set of ideas may be internally consistent, and compatible with the known facts, and still be dead and useless. Hence in learning to identify the truth one needs to look beyond these standard criteria. Not, however, I suggest, toward another criterion but to the ideal implicit in these.

In the last analysis, an idea is living and important only so far as it brings one into relationship with himself and with reality, so far as it "pulls things together." What is implied by the standards of logical consistency and factual accuracy is that nothing must be suppressed, nothing denied. An idea has the function of bringing one into relationship with reality. It is a bad idea if holding it requires one to ignore other things that he knows or believes. A true idea is one that helps to draw everything together into a comprehensible whole.

Feeling necessarily has a great part in the application of this ideal. One may check an idea against known facts and other ideas. The trouble is that much that must be pulled together does not have the definite and conscious form of a fact or an idea. A great idea is one that brings together and clarifies countless undefined memories and desires. It is the idea that does this that is "exciting." This may seem an invitation to believe whatever is pleasant or interesting. It must therefore be added that thinking tries one's depth and honesty. A great idea is one that draws together all that one finds in his experience and emotions when he searches without sentimentality or carelessness or fear.

Index